YVAN RIOUX was alrea(boy, taught by Christian I He studied biology at M. left him cold as it didn t touch anything that was alive. Working for ten years as a biodynamic farmer in Quebec, however, he encountered living ecosystems. Later, in Montreal, he taught on the relationship between human physiology and nature. In 1992 he moved to England with his two boys and joined a family of two girls and their mother, Gabriel Millar, who became his muse. Retiring ten years ago, he decided to write about his knowledge gained from 25 years of teaching experience, culminating in the publication of *The Mystery of Emerging Form*.

THE MYSTERY OF EMERGING FORM

Imma von Eckardstein's Drawings of the Constellations

A Biological Perspective

Yvan Rioux

TEMPLE LODGE

Temple Lodge Publishing Ltd.
Hillside House, The Square
Forest Row, RH18 5ES

www.templelodge.com

First published by Temple Lodge Publishing in 2017

A CIP catalogue record for this book is available from the British Library

ISBN 978 1 912230 02 0

Cover by Morgan Creative
Typeset by DP Photosetting, Neath, West Glamorgan
Printed and bound by 4Edge Ltd., Essex

Contents

Acknowledgements

Many thanks:

to my wife, the writer Gabriel Millar, who ruthlessly edited and opened me to the grammar and beauty of the English language (my mother-tongue is French);

to my son, Mathieu, the patient computer wizard, who provided inestimable instructions on technology and for his brilliant contribution to the organization of the text;

to my friend, Peter Stephenson, for our never-ending discussions about spiritual science where the thinking process is fed not only by outer perceptions but, more importantly, by inner ones;

and numerous other companions of my life for their encouragement.

Introduction

Any physiologist can tell you that our human organs are in a constant process of being broken down and rebuilt every second of our life. The material states (solid, liquid, gas and heat) move in and out of us without rest. Only the form and its function have a kind of permanency. We are recreated all the time inside vast rhythms. Life is before everything else rhythmic in its manifestation.

Every cell in our body is recycled and yet our form and the form of each organ and system is maintained. This remains one of the great mysteries of modern-day biology. What creates and influences the shape and the form of living entities?

There was a brief hope of an answer regarding the origin of forms in the 1960s with the discovery of the DNA double helix. Scientists realized very quickly that though they know more about the building of organic substances in each cell, the discovery of DNA did not reveal at all how these substances are bound into specific lines of force for the constant emergence of internal and external forms.

One thing is clear, for plants and animals, all their varied forms always start in a similar way as one germinal cell. The 'Human Genome Project' revealed 20,000 genes in our chromosomes which are fewer genes than many plant species (such as rice). So more genes does not necessarily mean more complex or evolved.

Our Own Creativity

As self-conscious beings we can observe our own creative activity. If a sculptor has the intention to create a human form, he will have to go through a specific process. The artist's idea will progressively turn into images of position, size, type of material etc. He might try some drawings, talk or read about it. It is a stage of image creation. These images crafted with intention can be stored a long time in his mind. In order for this form to appear in space he will need to gather materials, tools and human competence in a workshop. Here everything is vibrating, noisy and sweaty. Then through a rhythmic time process the form appears progressively in space.

The Greek philosopher and scientist Aristotle (384–322 BCE) was very interested in this process. He called the intention the 'final cause', whereas the image stage is more the 'formal cause'. As for the noisy aspect it is more the 'moving cause' and finally the achieved form is the 'material cause'.

This example is valid for any kind of creation we actualize in daily life, be it starting a course or going on holiday. It always starts with an intention. If that is how we actualize and create in our ordinary life, and we are, in our physical form a product of evolution, it is likely that the whole world manifestation proceeds in the same way. According to many religions' beliefs we are an image of God's intention.

This suggests that there is no separation between the creator and the created, between the thing observed and the formation of concept. The concept that emerges in our consciousness out of our perception is an aspect of the thing observed. They are not two separate worlds: one outside called nature and another one inside called psyche. The concepts of things emerging in our psyche are an integral part of the Beings of Things we observe.

This idea bears thinking about for a moment because it runs so counter to the central premise of objectivity so important to modern science. It tells us that it is impossible to be an objective observer because our very observation directly influences that which we are observing.

Steiner in his introduction of Goethe's *Theory of Colours* reminded us that human knowledge is not a process created inside a subject and disconnected from outside things: 'What emerges in our mind under the form of natural law, what manifests into our soul, it is the pulsation of the Universe itself.'

These concepts arise very early in our childhood like a primitive subconscious clairvoyance. Our psychic activity is co-functional with what we observe. It is obvious by simple observation of our life, and prior to any mental representation, that there is a world outside us in a constant process of becoming and passing away, like us, and its rhythmic aspect reverberates in us. As outside, so inside.

Aristotle called this way of seeing things hylomorphism where beings and things (*ousia*) are compounds of matter and form emerging out of nature's rhythms. Our perception of outside things includes, amongst other aspects, space, shape, colour, flavour and texture. Our sense perceptions bring an actuality as opposed to what it was before as potentiality. For our own physiology the smell of onion is a potential. When you enter into sense contact with it, it becomes actual. You notice the power of that energy on your eyes and nose. Every sense perception interacts with our consciousness and has a formative impact on our make-up. In this formative experience there is an agent (you), a conscious intelligent entity. Aristotle called this active spirit directing matter into form an entelechy — being in a certain state of perfection within (from the Greek *en*: within, *telos*: end, perfection, *Ekhein*: be in a certain state). *In this text the word 'spirit' means a conscious intelligent activity or intention that makes the fabric of the kingdoms of nature.* We can have great admiration for a type of building and marvel at the craftsmanship behind it and praise the architect who created the blueprint, and also the one who had the original intention for it. At these four levels of human creation we have various qualities of intelligences. The whole creation of forms in nature is not different.

Living Intentions

In this way of looking the whole cosmos is seen as purring with living intentions. The earth has its own regulatory activities auspicious to the manifestation of living species. Biologists observing living creatures continually encounter a multitude of well-balanced inner regulatory systems all dancing a complex rhythmic choreography. They observe the same thing for the earth and created the Gaia hypothesis inviting inter-disciplinary researches to encompass this holistic view.

Our earth is nested into the complex rhythms of the solar system with planets sending their influences in the form of loopy choreographic spheres. Everything is linked together with a rhythmic purpose. It is time to go beyond the atheistic notion of evolution by chance and necessity (random mutation and natural selection).

Our solar system is inside an even bigger system: the Milky Way galaxy. As we are within this galaxy's disc shape, when we look at the night sky we see it as a white band of denser stars encircling the earth. In the Western tradition, our forefathers divided the myriad of visible stars along this band into twelve sections or constellations. To these constellations they gave names and symbols. They were also aware of subtle influences emanating from these groups of stars. This study looks at the formative powers coming from these constellations and what impact these have on the physical form of living beings. Constellations and planets are physical aspects of the primal architects of the original intention, all bringing their own building impulses.

Our minds in freedom can accept or refute the existence of such an active impact with its own forms of intelligence — deities or formative forces. Aristotle imagined the whole cosmos as a gigantic rhythmic living organism that interacts with and constantly influences the physical world.

This text is trying to grasp the way these constellations express themselves in numerous ways from physical elements to animal and human constructions. We can believe in these relationships and learn them by heart or reject them as impossible to connect. But if we can succeed to articulate a link between them, we may come closer to an understanding of how these powers behind the stars are acting in nature.

The German writer and scientist Johann Wolfgang von Goethe (1749–1832) was one of the first in Western culture who said to the newly born scientific community that they should stop looking only at things and start to look at the Beings of Things. We can learn a lot through studying smaller and smaller parts of living creatures but the mystery of form with its specific function is never solved that way. As far as external animal forms are concerned, we can identify twelve common denominators between them in spite of their huge varieties. These denominators are vectors of activity on which the constellations have influences and which we will explore in this text.

To understand the form of our own internal organs and their metabolic processes we have to turn our gaze towards the planetary spheres. This study is mainly concerned with the external forms of animals and human beings.

'When man found how the world endlessly fragments into atoms, his perception bound itself with the death of nature; now he should strive to find what ends fragmentation and then his gaze will turn to the world's evolving growth.'[1] By doing so we might have a better idea of the sculptor behind it. Each constellation in the zodiac seems to offer a gesture that is essential in the material manifestation of life.

Imma's Drawings as a Starting Point

'Matter is the end of the ways of God.'[2]

'It was possible only for a highly developed soul to have provided such a definition of matter, which corresponds clearly to what Spiritual Science knows—such a definition is possible only from one who was in position to understand how the Divine spiritual creative forces function and focus to bring about a material structure as a human being, who in form is the expression of an enormous concentration of forces.'[3]

This exploration of the zodiac formative forces uses French artist, Imma von Eckardstein's drawings as a template to gather the various expressions of the constellations. These new motifs of the constellations were made in collaboration with Austrian philosopher, Rudolf Steiner (1861–1925) and developed further after Imma's death in 1930 by Margot Rossler over 30 years. They were originally published in *The Calendar of the Soul* in 1912.

> Imma von Eckardstein was born in Luneville, near Nancy [France] on November 5th 1871. She came into a family who had clairvoyant faculties in their ancestry. She was gifted with these faculties and was also an artist. At nineteen she went to study with the German painter and writer Josef Rolletscheck (1859–1934) in Weimar, Germany. There she met Steiner who was a friend of Rolletscheck. In 1911 Imma von Eckardstein asked Steiner about the possibility of a Theosophical — Anthroposophical calendar that could be the expression of the Consciousness Soul. Steiner gave her private lessons in Earth Evolution and its relation to inner training.[4]

> Steiner had entrusted a special task to the lady artist. Daily she was to meditate on the rising sun — rising for weeks at a time before one constellation after the other. For when the human being is able to do this, an 'intuitive picture' (so Dr Steiner calls it in the Foreword of the *Calendar of the Soul*) will dawn upon his soul — a picture in which the spiritual powers, living and moving in each constellation, find expression. Through such activity the Microcosm, man, is awakened. If Christ is the soul's guide, this will now speak out of the human soul.[5]

An 'intuitive' drawing of the kind that Imma produced can touch the human soul in many ways and be subject to many readings. This text is one reading from a biological perspective.

> We may take it as a favourable karma of our movement in Central Europe that we have such a personality among us. That this karma has a yet deeper foundation, we can see from the fact that the same person was able to cooperate so successfully in all that has been done, for instance, for our *Calendar* during the past months. Like all our understanding it is to serve the great purpose. So first among those who were able to collaborate in such an outstanding manner, not only as players but in the whole of our work, we may mention Fräulein von Eckardstein.[6]

One of the pioneers of quantum theory suggests that we should 'cross out that old word "observer" and put in its place the new word "participator"' co-evolving with the whole of nature.[7] Observation is the first step in scientific enquiry and then we hypothesize, experiment, find properties that have technological or medical application.

The constant advances of scienctific and technological discoveries regarding the properties of matter are coming faster than ever and are mesmerizing. Nevertheless, the properties of the material world remain mysterious. Every time a new one emerges, it is like discovering another aspect of a personality.

This study starts with the constellation Cancer and goes anticlockwise through the circle of the zodiac, like the path of the sun. So we study the simplest one-celled animals first and, progressively tracing evolution, make our way towards warm-blooded mammals in Leo.

The Layout of the Twelve Chapters is as Follows:

Preamble
At the beginning of each chapter we treat a subject relevant to this overall study. This preamble is not always directly connected with the chapter.

Imma's drawings
Each chapter presents Imma's drawing of the constellation with a brief 'Content' showing the multiple guises in which the constellation appears to our senses. At the bottom of each drawing the glyph of the constellation is shown.

Glyphs and Traditional Pictures
We will examine the glyph or symbol and the traditional medieval picture. These glyphs are not arbitrary emblems but come from a long tradition. There is a meaning in them that grasps the essence of the constellation. The glyph is shown at the bottom of each of Imma's drawings. One form of the twelve traditional

representations is expressed in the picture of this introduction. They express activities more than things, animals or human forms. Some twelfth century reproductions of the twelve zodiac signs are present in Audrey E. McAllen's book *The Listening Ear* and come from the Hunterian Psalter (M S Hunter 229) in Glasgow University Library.

A Scrutinizing Look at Imma's Drawing
A descriptive commentary of Imma's drawing will follow as a template for the rest of the study.

Exploring the Elements
Starting with the mineral kingdom we will investigate the activity of the element associated with that constellation inside living creatures.[8] Ever since the constellations were first described, mystics and scientists have sought to associate them with elements, symbols and temperaments or particular qualities. These associations were not made arbitrarily and reveal a search for deeper truths as to the constellations' influence on the formative forces active on our lives.

In the mineral kingdom the existence of substance is obvious. In the living kingdoms substances are continually 'becoming' — the 'process' accompanies the substance. When we examine living phenomena, we characterize the substances by their activities. Where there is life there are exchanges, transformations. Life manifests in the constant rhythmic metamorphosis of substance. A rhythmical unfolding where the four states of matter (solid, liquid, gas, heat) flow in and out organizing the physical life of living creatures.

Elements are drawn to one another like male and female. They bond to other elements and have preferences like us. The common model is that some are more inclined to donate electrons while others take them. This reactivity creates a bond that can be firm or loose like table salt when dissolved in water. This is the basic duality of the world and only one of the properties of the studied element. What scientists do is to observe the multiple properties of each element and apply them (in medicine or technology, for instance). But these properties are mysterious. We can't predict them but only discover them with observed trials. This is empiricism. It is not very different from seeing an unknown seed for the first time. We can't predict the way it will develop. We have to let it grow and observe the movement that reveals a typical root, leaf and flower.

A Plunge Into the Animal Kingdom
Through the work of Austrian- German physician Eugen Kolisko (1893–1939) and others on the twelve animal phyla associated with the constellations we can study the type of each phylum in relation with the drawing.[9]

The Ways our Senses Perceive the World
Steiner linked each constellation with a specific sensory capability, and we look at each of them in connection with an animal phylum.[10]

One Part of our Body Structure
The medieval tradition also links each constellation with a specific human body area. These links were reiterated by Steiner's investigation (Fig. 1.). It is a bad habit of the modern intellect to discard ancient knowledge as something that has no foundation. We sometimes see ancient traditions as quaint or ignorant until we realize that they understood or described a deeper truth. We will look at the anatomical influence of each constellation on the human body.

The Planetary Sphere that rules the Constellation
We will look at the formative metabolic impact the planetary spheres have on specific constellations' influences when entering the solar system. These seven spheres of influence (Moon, Mercury, Venus, Sun, Mars, Jupiter, Saturn) are like filters for the gifts that come from the twelve star groupings of the Milky Way. The term planetary spheres refers to the mobile bodies dancing around the earth when viewed from a geocentric vantage and

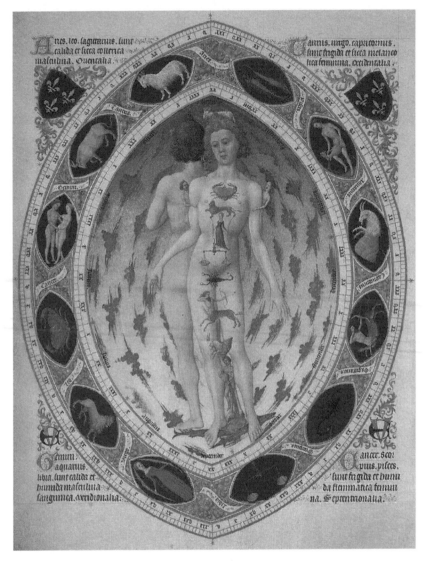

Fig. 1 This fifteenth century picture of constellations and body parts comes from Les Très Riches Heures du Duc de Berry

was first described by the Greek Ptolemy in the second century BCE. These expressions include the Sun and the Moon, all the planets up to Saturn. Uranus, Neptune and Pluto have an impact more on our psyche with its soul faculties (thinking, feeling, willing). It is with these faculties that man's spirit transforms his animality. In this study these seven planetary spheres will be mentioned briefly as metabolic processes.

The Consonant Formative Impact Related to the Constellation

The consonants[11] are formative for the embryonic brain in early childhood. Babies start with vowels and gradually, through imitation, develop the muscular capacity to pronounce consonants.

'The more the child moves beyond the vowels formed in mere crying and utters consonants such as L, M, N, R, the more the left cerebral convolution is structured in an artful way.'[12]

In so many ways a child learns through imitation. The production of consonants develops and co-ordinates the various muscles of the face, larynx and abdomen.

'Just as a carver shapes a piece of wood [...] so the child's [muscular] movements "sculpt" the brain. The organs the child moves carry their movement right into the brain. If I want to pronounce L, I have to use my tongue. The tongue is connected with the brain through nerves and through other organs. This L penetrates into my cerebral convolution and produces a structure there [...] M produces spherical circumvolutions'[12] This is the Broca area of the (mainly) left frontal hemisphere essential for speech production.

'So you see, these sounds work on the brain.'[12]

During that formative early childhood period, hearing a language is essential for future understanding of written or spoken words. The development of the Wernicke's area of the left temporal lobe is done at an early age by listening to a language. If no language is spoken for the first two to three years of a baby's life it will be very difficult in the future for him to develop the capacity to speak.

Attractive Colours for the Soul

To have a grasp of colours[13] we need to use our feeling intelligence.

If we organize the seven colours of the rainbow in a circle and let the red hot side play with the cool blue side, then five new hues of mingled blue and red (violet) emerge. Many artists work with this circle of twelve colours (seven plus five) often associated with the twelve constellations.

When the eye perceives a colour, it enters immediately into activity, and, because of its nature, produces on the visual field another colour, as much unconscious as necessary. These two colour experiences, the conscious and the unconscious, tend to reconstruct the totality of the chromatic experience. We can experience these two by focussing for a while on yellow and then placing our gaze on a white paper. An after-image of blue-red (violet) is produced in our internal visual field when we close our eyes. The primary colour (yellow) excites the production of the other primary colours.

Each of the twelve constellations has its own colour. In this text the colours associated with the constellations will be named *but only the green of Cancer will be explored briefly*.

'... the world man inhabits between death and a new birth ... is a soul permeated, spirit permeated world of light, of colour, of sound, ... '[14]

The Constellation's Eurythmy Gesture Reflecting our Psychic Life

The eurythmy gestures of the constellations[15] were given by Steiner and *only the one for Cancer will be described here*. These gestures summarize, in their essence, the impact of the constellations on our psyche. They remind us that we have a psychic life with its three forms of intelligence (thinking, feeling and willing) acting in tandem for the realization of a spirit's destiny on earth. They range from the enthusiastic (Leo) impulse for action, through to reflection on the consequences of the fait accompli.

'We should see the eurythmy as direct reproduction of the relation between a human being with the [forces of the] cosmic periphery.'[16]

Conclusion

A conclusion will accompany each chapter.

In summary

All these associations may seem a bit odd but are diverse aspects of the Beings of the constellations.

Is it possible to find a golden thread between them that can give us a clearer picture of these formative rhythmic activities ever present in our surroundings?

> ... the fact that man, on passing through the gate of death, must surrender his physical body to the elements of the external, physical world: these destroy it. The action of the external nature upon the human physical body is destructive, not constructive. So we must look quite outside the physical world for what gives the human physical body its shape between birth (or conception) and death. We must speak, to begin with, of another world which builds up this human body that external Nature can only destroy.[17]

Many of these associations were given by Steiner through numerous lectures and developed later by his scientific and artistic followers. All twelve constellations work in tandem in all the animal phyla, but each one brings its own vector of activity to the specific twelve animal groups. In his external form man embodies an embryonic summary of all the phyla. Imma's drawings awaken a desire to approach these creative forces in a new way and help us to grasp the twelve main impulses of the original architects in the mineral, plant and animal kingdoms. The embryos of mammals, birds and man are very similar at the beginning. The original embryonic shoulder buds specialize into wings for birds whereas the horses' four legs end up walking on the nail of the middle fingers (hoofs). Contrary to the animals specialization, man's limbs are unspecialized and, therefore, capable of many complex actions.

Many new terms representing cell types and structures or

primitive phyla species are offered in this text. Because of the easy access to the Internet it is strongly recommended that the reader do his own search if he wants to visualize these terms through images.

1. Cancer

Preamble

In numerous ways through his work Rudolf Steiner attracted our attention to the constant, ever-present activity of the spirit world for the emergence of life (immanence) in nature. For instance, in most translations of Christ's prayer the first sentence is 'Our Father Who art in heaven' which orients us towards a trans-cendent Being. In Steiner's rewriting of this prayer—'Father, you Who were, are, and will be in the inmost being of all'[1]—we are more in touch with His ever-present aspect. Considering the fact that the living kingdoms are constantly reshaping their form, we can expect a continual flow of formative forces raining down on our planet all the time informing the spirits in incarnation.

In the manifestation of these formative forces or beings '...Goethe rather means that one should not speak at all of hidden being. The being is not behind its manifestation. On the contrary, it comes into view through manifestation. This being, however, is in many respects so rich that it can manifest itself to other senses in still other forms. What reveals itself does belong to the being, but because of the limitation of our senses it is not the whole being.'[2]

This is the key sentence to summarize this book. The aim of which is to overcome this limitation and show the way the beings of these formative forces act constantly in the kingdoms of nature. When scientists want to define what is alive do they really understand the dynamic through which forms emerge in space from within?

It is obvious that all living creatures emerge from a very small point, a germinal cell and develop from inside out in space through a time process. Who is using this nucleic genetic set of keys in order to create a living form? There is a need for a presence, a consciousness to build these complex carbohydrate (plant) or protein (animal) architectures.

As with every archeological monument we sense an intelligent activity working with purpose and not a random assemblage of carved stones. Why do we not orient our mind in the same way towards all forms in the living kingdoms?

Nuclear physicists fragment matter in search of the ultimate particle, whereas astronomy has reduced the earth to an insignificant speck of dust in the infinite vastness of the galactic universe.

On the other hand religious people of all kinds try to confront modern science by denying the modelling of their theory of evolution. In their critique they are not entirely wrong pointing out the inadequacy of this model. Some stick to Genesis literally. At the same time they don't notice the six days described in Genesis. Read the first six days and it is obvious that it is describing an evolutionary process where man in his physicality appears on the sixth day. Days in this context represent a period of time and are not meant literally as 24 hours. Whereas others adopt the idea that their gods, the primal

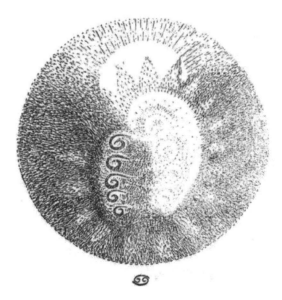

Drawing of the Constellation of Cancer (Crab)

movers, acted at the start of Creation and retired on the seventh day.

Is it not time to step beyond these two tendencies? One invites us to believe that Creation, without purpose, comes out of the random activity of atoms, whereas the other one sees a purposeful Creation as a complex choreography of spiritual Beings (Hierarchies) acting at the beginning, but now at rest (the seventh day), letting matter's given laws and properties generate the various kingdoms of nature. Nevertheless we may suppose that the material and spiritual co-evolve all the time.

Content

This text explores the imprint of the intelligent activity of Cancer's presence all around us in the constant formation of humans and animals. What is the link between the Cancer sector of space, its glyph, the medieval image of this constellation, Imma's drawing, the element phosphorus, the animal phylum Protozoa, the sense of touch, the thorax, the Moon as a ruling sphere, the colour green, the consonant F and an eurythmy gesture? Based on Imma von Eckardstein's drawings, published in the first edition of *The Calendar of the Soul* in 1912, we can try to find a golden thread linking the various ways Cancer acts as a blueprint in nature.

Description of the Glyph and the Traditional Picture

The Cancer glyph suggests an inner space delineated by two curved lines open to outer space. It shows a force that envelops and protects a space while still open to the outside.

It is understandable that the traditional crab image was used to represent Cancer. All plants have a sensitivity, and all animals a sensoriality with regard to their milieux. They all have specific rhythmic pulses and a capacity to transform the outer world of nature generating a new creation (metabolism + movement + reproduction). These three functions (this threefoldness) in the crab are compressed into a single lump. In the reptile group we have a similar form expression with the turtle. Most animals tend to develop specific body parts (head, thorax and abdomen) as centres of these activities: perception, rhythmic pulse and transformation. These basic activities are also found in each organ if we really want to penetrate its secrets.

Description of the Drawing

With the sun in the background looking more like a sunrise shooting its light on a misty dense surrounding, it is possible to imagine an early earth phase where all the water was in a vapour state because the ground was just too hot. Giant electric storms rained down for aeons on this proto-earth progressively lifting the heat out into the cosmos. Hundreds of kilometres of misty water, with varying degrees of heat, formed a gaseous globe filled with living forces.

'There was at the earth periphery where today we have the atmosphere, something like a fine liquid, intermediary between water and the actual atmosphere. This subtle liquid was analogous to albumin.'[3] We can imagine it as a warm milky fog giving birth to the beginning of organic life.

Central to this drawing we have the archetypal form of an embryonic beginning, a germ (seed or cell) entering into the realm of matter. Our attention is directed towards the boundary of this germ where clockwise whirling pulsations cross this boundary and become anticlockwise. We then have an inner space with a boundary membrane where the interior relates with the exterior. The reversal of these whirls shows an impulse of individualization inside this little space, a bit like the food we dismantle during digestion before building our own protein substance. On the left side we notice another radiating structure in formation. Is it the birth of a new cell?

An enclosed space is one of the basic features of all living creatures. Be it bark, skin or a cellular membrane, it is essential for a functioning organism to have its privacy. Even inside us, because each organ has a special task to perform with regards to the whole, each one is isolated inside membranes e.g. pericardium (heart) and meninges (brain). In society we notice this tendency too, be it a house for a family or the boundary of a country.

Phosphorus: Opening the Gate of Incarnation

Which element helps the most to enclose a tiny drop of liquid for life to start? Phosphorus is a good candidate when we look into the intimate nature of a membrane and its phospholipid unit.

Phosphorus is Cancer in the mineral kingdom. We will look now at the places where we find this substance and its properties in living creatures. But first, it is a known fact that phosphorus can capture light, hold it for a while and give it away again. Often alarm clocks have a bit of it on their hands that allows us to see the time in the dark — phosphorescence.

Phosphorus in us is abundant in our bone structure linked with calcium (calcium phosphate). The phosphate concentration is maintained in the blood stream by hormones from glands around the larynx and is instrumental in gathering the basic bimolecular layer of phospholipids of all cell membranes (plants and animals) at the start of their life on earth.

'Phosphorus made the earth an avid planet that attracts to her the ingredients of the cosmos.'[4]

The architectural ingredients of the cell (organelles) need a private enclosure to manifest. Phosphorus, by caging a tiny drop of the ocean, brings into this new interiority the possibility for a spirit to manifest its form from inside out.

In the drawing the whole germ radiates light that surrounds the seed as if sunlight is imprisoned or enchanted inside. The light bearer, phosphorus, is not only instrumental in generating cellular membrane; it provides the main tools for the capture and transport of energy when sugar is burnt in the furnace (mitochondria) of each cell (adenosine mono, di and triphosphate or AMP/ADP/ATP—another organic form of phosphorus).[5] In this organic form phosphorus is a holder and carrier of sunlight energy inside the cell, essential for all metabolic activities.

Bacteria and Protozoa: Simplest of Living Creatures

The smallest group of one-celled creatures is called the fermenters or bacteria, the most ancient of which is cyanobacteria which has both plant and animal characteristics. Bacteria are the digestive system of the earth and responsible for the dismantlement of rocks. They are everywhere and live in symbiosis with all other living creatures. Through endosymbiosis they form the energy organelle of more complex cells (mitochondria in animals and chloroplasts in plants with a genetic code different from their hosts).[6]

French scientist Paul Portier was the first, in 1918, to offer the hypothesis that mitochondria and chloroplasts descend from bacteria. American biologist Lynn Margulis (1938–2011) and her son, the science writer Dorion Sagan, in their book *The Microcosm,* added interesting results from their bacterial research. Their hypothesis of endosymbiosis (incorporating the bacteria as organelles) is now becoming more accepted in the scientific community. They are much smaller than the Protozoa and have simpler forms. If a normal cell in the human body is blown up to the size of a family home, the bacteria are the size of the front door. Nevertheless we can't live without them. They live at the border of our little empire by the hundreds of millions—in our skin and gut—and their fermenting activities are vital for our well-being. This is what symbiosis is all about—both profit from this essential association. Nevertheless our immune system resists their potential intrusion (they must stay at the border). There are always barbarians at the edge of any empire.

If they appeared on earth long before plants and animals, what were they fermenting? To understand this we must imagine the primeval atmosphere on earth during the Hadean and Archean eras (4.5 billion to 2.5 billion years ago). Abundant hydrogen reacted with carbon to form methane, with oxygen to form water, with sulphur to give hydrogen sulphide and nitrogen to generate ammonia, etc. Cyanide, formaldehyde, and many other gases, were probably part of this ancient mixture.

Add to this: molten lava bombarded by meteorite rain and every imaginable electromagnetic radiation from the cosmos; millions of years of violent electrical storms, when the fallen water steamed up constantly, took more heat out into the cosmos, cooling the surface. Imagine all the water on earth as hundreds of kilometres of clouds in the atmosphere. Then continental plates in constant movement, creating earthquakes and volcanic activity, started to appear in parallel with a primeval muddy ocean soup. The earth was cooling off.

> The Miller-Urey experiments in 1953 were germinal. Since then almost every simple compound (amino acids …) of complex cell molecules has been produced in the lab. Today several basic compounds have been produced by sending electric sparks or ultraviolet, etc. through various mixtures of simple gases and mineral solutions. Luckily, the four most abundant amino acids in the proteins of all organisms are the most easily formed. The indispensable compound adenosine triphosphate (ATP), a molecule that stores energy inside the cell, and other triphosphate precursors of the nucleotides (the structural basis of genes) can also be formed by this sort of experiment. So it is likely that progressively, a pre-biotic chemistry began in the atmosphere.[7]

'Biologists are obliged to suppose that the environment where the first life forms appeared, and where biogenesis was possible, must have been itself, in a certain sense, living.'[8]

So what we have here is a fertile milky atmosphere, the structure and forces of which allowed the intervention of a creative intelligence in the different living kingdoms that will emerge from it.

In 1923 Steiner spoke about this primeval atmosphere in the cycle 'Centres of Ancient Mysteries', where he described this atmosphere as a very fine liquid, something between liquid and gas, like albumen. Later, with the cooling off of the earth, as it reached the solid state and life ether level, this albumen started to differentiate into diverse elements that today we call carbon, hydrogen, oxygen, nitrogen, etc. That whole milky atmosphere was penetrated by this cosmic ether (formative forces) that animated the milk.

The penetration of this original milk by etheric formative forces from the centre of the galaxy is not recognized in science today. The methodology of modern science is not equipped to understand these super-sensible forces. (See Preamble of chap. 5.) As long as modern science refuses to recognize these forces, scientists will never be able to understand the mysteries of the living form.

In this milky warm atmosphere bacteria were born, creating, by their fermenting function, new earth conditions to allow more elaborate forms to incarnate. They were fermenting this original milk — think of intestinal chyme, a substance that we generate every day in our digestive system.

Bacteria are called prokaryotes because their genetic material is not inside a nuclear membrane but free in the cytoplasm. As English scientist James Lovelock says in *Gaia*:

> These tiny organisms are complete: they can exchange matter and energy with their environment, maintain a constant size and composition, and reproduce by mitosis. They come in all shapes and sizes from the spheres of the cocci to the rods of the bacilli and the thin spirals of the spirochetes. Some swim free, propelled by slender fibres that thrash the fluid of their medium like tiny oars, while others are less mobile: the sarcina bunched in cubes like the atoms of crystals; the staphylococci growing like bunches of grapes; the streptococci in chains.

With the invention of the microscope and other laboratory techniques, scientists have worked hard in the last 100 years to identify different species of bacteria. Nevertheless, in spite of various forms and functions of bacteria, many scientists today are of the opinion that all bacteria are one species scattered everywhere because they can all exchange genetic material.

The simplicity of their free-floating chromosomes (hundreds of thousands of pairs of genes compared to millions in plants and animals) allows a great plasticity in the exchange of genes. This is also why they can adapt quickly to changes or aggressions in their environment. We all know the immense problems medicine now has with some bacteria now capable of resisting all known antibiotics. Bacteria can survive extreme conditions and live a long time by contracting into seeds.

The Numerous One-Celled Animals

Protozoa: Numerous Species

After the emergence of bacteria, there came bigger one-celled creatures in the muddy primeval oceans. Again a tiny drop of liquid isolated by a semi-permeable membrane is the start of all plants (algae) and animals (Protozoa). The oceans and lakes became auspicious for the development of greater expression. From prokaryotes (no nuclear membrane) we go to unicellular eukaryotes (the chromosomes are isolated in a nuclear membrane). In prokaryotes movement is very slow. In eukaryotes they tend to move faster in predetermined pathways organized by a tubular matrix. The inner activities show a rhythmical expansion and contraction. This is the beginning of species, and these newcomers were not going to lose the preceding expression of life. They simply incorporated the bacteria as organelles.

Here, according to Margulis, we are not talking about survival of the fittest but a rhythmic evolutionary process, where continual interaction, co-habitation, mutual dependency and networking matrices are the basis for the later appearance of the plant and animal kingdoms.[7]

One key characteristic of animals is movement. Even at this early stage various types of mobility emerge. The main types created by Protozoa will be reused by the multicelled organism and are still present in us to this day. These archetypal ways of behaving will be in the service of a new incarnated intelligence.

'The bodies of human beings and animals are composed of such a cell.'[9]

These primitive cells use their membranes in various ways. For the sake of mobility and prehension they extend their external skin into pseudopodia (Fig. 1). In us we have the macrophages of our immune cells. Some of them immobilize themselves to allow other movements like astrocytes, podocytes and oligodendrocytes.

Fig. 1 *Photo of a one cell amoeba showing his mobile extended membrane or Pseudopodia*

Astrocytes, part of the blood-brain barrier, are more responsible for the movement of feeding liquid around the neurons of our brain. They nurse and hold the scaffolding. They pulse to allow the virtual liquid to move around the neurons.

Podocytes on the other hand are fixed too, surrounding the capillaries in the glomerular capsule of each nephron in our kidneys. They become filters for the movement of blood serum at the start of urine formation.

Like astrocytes (star cells), the oligodendrocytes are also part of the connective tissue of the nervous system (neuroglia). They enrol their membranes with phospholipids around the neuron axons to favour the movement of nervous influx. It is called the myelin sheath and is under development in young children as long as they are using their sensorial and motor apparatus.

Some other Protozoa create cilia (Fig. 2) like those in the lining of the bronchi of our lungs or generate and move the cerebrospinal fluid (ependymal cells) directly in touch with the grey matter of the brain. Still other Protozoa sport flagella (Fig. 3) as in the sperm cell. The membranes in some species also excrete a sophisticated external skeleton using silica such as in Radiolaria

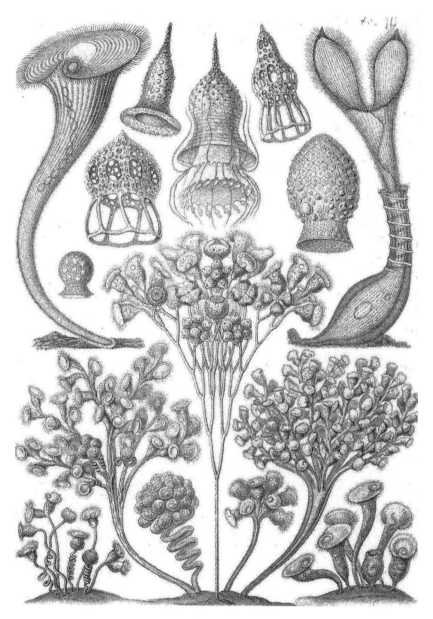

Fig. 2 Drawing of one-celled ciliate

(Fig. 4) or calcium in the Foraminifera (Fig. 5). This is what the osteocytes of our bones are doing all the time – secreting minerals and fibres.

Those who believe that complexity of form depends on

Fig. 3 Drawing of one-celled flagellate

pluricellular organisms are in for a surprise when they look at the different species of Protozoa. These are amazingly complex and beautiful in their movement and structure.

The Foraminifera (Fig. 5) are shaped more like animals (e.g.

Fig. 4 Drawing of one-celled Radiolaria (silica external excretion)

molluscs and snails), whereas Radiolaria are closer to the kingdom of plants and minerals and are essentially porous animals
(Fig. 4).

The one-cell cilia and flagellates are also quite amazing in their

Fig. 5 Drawing of one-celled Foraminifera (calcium external excretion)

Figs. 2 to 5 are drawings by Ernst Haeckel, biologist, made at the end of the nineteenth century

refined designs. At the end of the nineteenth century, German biologist Ernst Haeckel (1834–1919) made drawings of invertebrates that can be found in his wonderful book *The Art Forms of Nature* (Dover Publication Inc). Highly recommended.

For aeons, by their constant sedimentation, they were forming rocks contributing to the clarification of the primitive ocean.

'The compressed mud of Foraminifera can be seen in the chalk of the cliffs of Dover.'[9]

To this day they are still doing this, and their forms express an aspect of future multicellular phyla. This is the start of the exoskeleton—a capacity to extract and harden a mineral into amazing forms.

At the level of unicellular living units, we have animals with chlorophyll, moving or not, and creatures like plants with animal characteristics. Later the plant cells will develop cellulose shields and become more rigid, whereas some pluricellular animals will have plant shapes, like the marine sponges.

'Plant and animal qualities are intermingled in one and the same individual in many protozoa.'[7]

The Sense of Touch: Membrane Sensitivity

This is the sense attributed to the constellation of Cancer. After all, our skin is the first to show us that we have an interiority. As a major area of exchange between an inside and an outside, the external membrane or skin is always very sensitive to its environment. The sense of touch[10] starts here with high sensitivity (plants) and sensoriality (organ sensors) in animals. Later in more developed animals this external membrane will involute in the embryo (ectoderm) to give birth to the central nervous system (the brain is an involuted skin) bringing a more conscious sensoriality. The same phospholipids that isolate and give surface sensitivity are found around the nerves as the myelin sheath for better influx transmission.

An Enclosure Guarding a Pulsing Centre: Thoracic Cage

The drawing of Cancer by Imma shows very well the enclosing power of this constellation. This simple cavity holding light is the precursor of the future thorax — the main pulsing centre in the more evolved animals. Cancer doesn't provide the pulse. Without an intelligent entity in a house bringing a pulsing activity nothing happens in it. So it is for the enormous varieties of living creatures with their complex forms and movements. An entelechy[11] is in action here using the equipment given by the formative aspect of the stars.

Moon Sphere Rules Cancer

Another darker form irradiating light in Imma's drawing can be seen to the left of the whirls. It is like a birthing process. The moon rules Cancer and its metabolic process is duplication (or mitosis). This cellular division insures the permanency of generation through cloning. It is with this basic enclosing equipment that the first unicellular living creatures (lit porous urn) started to manifest and duplicate (bacteria, Protozoa, etc.) with the help of all the other super-sensible forces.

In this early group we also have the beginning of a meiotic process where two parents are involved. This form of individuation of the genetic material depends more on the Scorpio constellation as we shall see later. Apart from our germinal cells, all our cellular divisions reproduce in a mitotic way. Again phosphorus is instrumental in the formation of nucleic acid — the basis of genetic material.

The Consonant F

This whirling activity at the boundary of the membrane can be seen as a blowing breath that activates the exchange between an inner and an outer world. We sound the consonant F associated with Cancer when we blow air to start a fire. The F sound flies away with a strong contraction of abdominal, 'will' muscles. In *The Creation of Adam* by Italian painter Michaelangelo (1475–1564) God gives his own fiery breath for Adam to become an autonomous being.[12]

The Colour Green

The colour green is associated with Cancer. To grasp this relation we have to leave the intellect and go to our feeling intelligence. Walking in an environment without any green — e.g. desert land — the soul experiences an absence of boundary, as though the soul could expand to infinity. It is an exhilarating sense of expansion without limit. On the other hand walking in a green landscape we feel enveloped and protected. The soul rests, satisfied. This is a representation of the Cancer impulse.

'The moral effect of green is to produce comfort and repose...'[13]

'Green is a denser colour, supportive and harmonious, that likes to limit itself. It is the colour of the living earth.'[14]

The Eurythmy Gesture

The right arm over the chest, the left arm over the back.

The arms envelop the central rhythmic area where the heart and lungs pulse. The spirit in incarnation dwells in the warm flow of the blood that generates the heartbeat. In this sanctum the blood flows into the heart and it is here that our intentional impulse to act emerges.

Conclusion

Cancer lends a periphery to each living unit, an intimate location where an intentional interiority (spirit) can manifest. This enclosure is clear in Imma's drawing.

In a nutshell, we have surveyed the enveloping power of this constellation creating unique interiority for creative spirits of all kinds to evolve their own rhythmic life in the realm of nature and play a role as organs of the biosphere. A highly sensitive membrane, by isolating a tiny drop of liquid, allows an intelligent presence to sense what is outside it. By being semi-permeable this membrane guarantees a minimum control of what goes in and out, which is essential for their new proteinic architectures to emerge. Just as we might take stones from the mountain to build a house, living creatures incorporate the substances of nature to build carbohydrate (plant) or proteinic architecture (animal).

From the membrane of the simplest cell to the most elaborate cavity (thorax), there is an impulse to generate an enclave, a porous vessel where, in the intimacy of an interior, a spirit can pulse and manifest its form.

The properties of Cancer's mineral manifestation (phosphorus) also give membranes sensitivity and the equipment to handle energy (ATP) in that tiny place.

In their inner urge for mobility they develop various types of movement still in use in the various phyla to this day. Protozoa extracted silica or calcium from the primeval muddy ocean to elaborate complex architecture, clarifying it by the sedimentation of their shells.

What would be the use of all this activity if they could not perpetuate? The moon impulse rules here and gives them the mitotic division: a possibility to clone or divide into two with exactly the same genetic material. A similar process is found in the budding of plants and early invertebrates.

In all, what a fantastic equipment for an intelligent entity to dwell in!

Whether we touch what we see or the mystery of what lies beneath the veil of what we see [Beings of Things], we are made for unending meeting and exchange, while having to hold a coherent mind and body, physically and imaginatively, which in turn can be found and touched itself. We are something for the World to run up and rub up against: through the trials of love, through pain, through happiness, through our simple everyday movement through the World.[15]

'... by wanting to get to know the structure of the World in all its aspects ... a kind of striving to know all the subtle aspects of cosmic happenings, we attain our higher ego by evolving from stage to stage.'[16]

2. Gemini

Preamble

The impact of Gemini on animal forms is seen in the next stage of evolution. We are now looking at cells loosely organized into tissues and heading more and more towards organ systems. If we are going from one-celled to pluricelled animals, it might be relevant to ask: What is a cell?

> A cell is something with a mind of its own that stands out against what the Human Being represents. It has its own way of growing, its own life. If you consider on the one hand the whole form of the human being as it has been fashioned by powers prevailing on this Earth and powers from beyond this Earth, and then somehow come to consider the cell, it is the cell which upsets the applecart for those primary powers. It actually destroys those external powers, wanting to develop a life of its own. Even under normal conditions we are constantly waging war in our organism against the life of the cell. The absurdest of views has arisen in connection with therapy and physiology at the cellular level, with the cell consistently regarded as the primary element and the human organism as a construct of cells. In reality the human being is a whole and as such connected with the Cosmos, and is forever involved in the struggle against the self-will of the cell. It is actually the cell which is constantly causing disruption in the organism; it does not play a constructive role.[1]

Cells are highly complex structures but so small we cannot see them. The development of various microscopic devices has allowed modern biologists to glimpse into this very complex and mesmerizing micro milieu with its various little organs (organelles). The usual fixed drawing of a cell misses many features that are not easy to show. It allows us to see only the forms of these tiny organs but not so much their complicated inter-relations.

In a time when scientific research is strongly focussed on

genes, scientists cannot explain the emergence of these organelles in the first Protozoa. Some of these little organs, such as mitochondria and centrioles, have their own genetic material different from their host. To focus only on gene manipulation of the chromosomes is to ignore 98 per cent of the genetic material present in the cell, usually called 'junk DNA'.

The following is a list of some important features not represented in the typical drawing of a cell:

1. Incorporated in the membrane we have a set of proteins that allows the active movement of specific substances. Some proteins are sensitive to hormonal influences that can change the cell metabolism. We also have on the surface of each cell protein markers (like fingerprints) as signs of our own individuality. That is why our immune cell can identify what is me and what is a stranger.

2. Inside a living cell there is an extremely complex matrix of fibres organizing all organelles for greater efficiency in producing protein. Cells are capable of building proteins so fast it still baffles biologists. This matrix of fibres is in touch with the surrounding connective tissue that separates and unifies all organs.

3. This nano drop of living technology (the cell) is doped with tiny quantities of co-factors (copper, zinc, magnesium ... and vitamins) that are essential to the speed at which the enzymes work. Some of these elements are so dilute that they act more as a process than a substance. The notion of 'doping' is not new or unknown to science: all the silicon in computer processors is 'doped' (with arsenic ...), and just a very small quantity is needed to change the silicon into a semiconductor.

4. Every cell is constantly emitting bio-photonic light coherent as a laser. Are we close to a new way of understanding how cells and tissues communicate? The subtle energy that circulates in the meridians is a kind of liquid light flowing through the body in a diurnal rhythm, formed by the

mingling of external and internal influences. How does it pulse in us? Because of its complex protein crystalline structure, the connective tissue of our body has semiconductive properties. If it is a semiconductor what does it carry?

To make sense of this complex organization we need to remember that every living unit or cell needs:

1. a boundary (membrane);
2. a centre of command (nucleus, nucleolus and centrosome);
3. a source of energy and defence (mitochondria and lysosomes);
4. a place of transformation (endoplasmic reticulum — Golgi apparatus, vesicles and vacuoles);
5. an agent of transformation (ribosomes).

We have here the essential component of any living unit of production. Human beings, like animals, have a protein architecture and their cells are designed to produce proteins, among other things. What is the goal of the intelligent activity of this living unit? Before we can answer this question, we need to identify and understand the five organs that are essential to the accomplishment of these tasks.

The creation of protein by a human cell can be compared simplistically on a macro scale to a brick factory, a restaurant or a hospital. We can apply this to all living units as long as we can answer the question: What is the function of this unit of production?

The Five Basic Requirements for the Functioning of a Living Unit

A Boundary:
The cell — a highly sensitive membrane that delimits an interiority with the possibility of an in-out exchange.

The brick factory — a highly sensitive perimeter with sophisticated fences, doors, windows etc ... allowing controlled in-out exchange.

A Centre of Command:

The cell — the nucleus has all the information to produce any kind of protein but uses only a fraction of its potential in our cells. For instance the islets of Langerhans in the pancreas sense the blood sugar level and produce hormones (insulin, glucagon) to establish the right balance. This centre of command of a cell is always meeting the demand of the organ or tissue. The centrosome/centriole linked with the nucleus is in charge of organizing the cellular division.

The brick factory — the office of the factory has the knowledge to produce all kinds of bricks, but creates only those types demanded by the builders in a specific area. If the demand for bricks is great, there is always the chance to enlarge the factory or build another one in another place (swarming process).

A Source of Energy and Defence:

The cell — sugar is burned in the mitochondria, freeing the sun energy to build proteins. Pockets of lysosomes (basic tool) used to digest and rebuild organic material, clean the internal space and eliminate intruders.

The brick factory — after being made with tools the furnace cooks the bricks using oil, gas or electricity, and there is also a surveillance system to defend, clean and maintain the factory site.

A Place of Transformation:

The cell — here the proteins are made (endoplasmic reticulum), packaged in the right way (Golgi apparatus) and excreted (vesicles). Basic materials coming from outside (amino acids etc...) are put into storage (vacuoles).

The brick factory — the production floor where the bricks are made, cooked and packaged for export or stored in the yard. Also where the primal material (clay or pigments) is stored.

An Agent of Transformation:

The cell — the ribosomes relay messages from the nucleolus to the cytoplasm to organize the production of proteins when they (ribosomes) are attached to the endoplasmic reticulum. The free ribosomes organize the matrix that links all the organelles inside the cell.

The brick factory — the foreman relays orders from the office to the factory floor and organizes the production.

When molecular biologists James Watson and Francis Crick discovered the double helix of DNA in the 1960s, scientists were confident that the mystery of forms would soon be unravelled. The discovery, in fact, showed only how the cell dismantles and reorganizes organic matter according to a genetic programme. This clever discovery doesn't account for the hundreds of types of cells and their assemblage into organs and tissues (form and function). The origin and formation of organs is still a mystery that can only be approached with the concept of the morphogenic field (as postulated by English biologist Rupert Sheldrake) or an area of space that has lines of forces able to organize matter. A magnet, for instance, is a morphogenic field for iron dust. In living creatures we are intuiting forces more in touch with the super-sensible world.

When we look at the way original cells (stem cells or mesenchyme) differentiate according to their location in the embryo, and at the huge reservoir of hormones necessary to control the metabolic processes in our cells, and how oncologists say that cancer occurs all the time in our body but our immune system (inner digestive system) gets rid of the cancer even before we notice it — then this definition of a cell by Steiner[1] starts to make sense. In this context cancer will predominate only in an area where the immune system doesn't operate properly because of lack of circulation, immune deficiency or toxins.

The cells in a pluricellular organism are obviously in service of a higher expression. The first animal cells (Protozoa), as we saw in Chapter One, created a functioning blueprint of inner activities (organelles) plus various types of movement. All the other phyla will reuse similar organelles and movements in the service of a new intelligent manifestation.

Whereas the outer form of animals depends more on the influence of the constellations, the metabolic processes of our inner organs depend more on the planetary spheres of activity. Rudolf Steiner in *Occult Physiology* as well as traditional Chinese physiology have a lot to say about this. But this is the subject of another book. This text is predominantly concerned with the external organization of animals and human beings.

From Tissues to Organ Systems

We observe a progression from a loose tissue assemblage of cells in early animals such as in the sponges (Porifera) towards a more complex system of organs in jellyfish (Coelenterata). To understand this progression, it is useful to ask: What is an organ?

Looking at an organ under the microscope we see a coordinated cooperation of tissues made of cells. All organs have neuro-sensorial and motor components, a certain rhythm and metabolic activities. How they appear is a much more difficult question. Observation confirms the fact that a specific locus in the embryo has a tremendous impact on these newly born stem cells (or mesenchyme) to the extent of orienting them towards the creation of a specific organ. The embryologist Rupert Sheldrake called it a morphogenic field. It seems that the organs are the final result of 'a system of forces working behind the outer appearances'.[2]

Once the organ is formed, and for the rest of our lives, this organ in its materiality will be constantly renewing itself. Facing that simple observable fact 'we can't look at an organ as a static form, but rather we should see it as a nodal point within a constant flow of coming into being and passing away again'.[3]

If we want to have an understanding of where, when and how they emerge in us, we need to observe the appearance and movement of the organs in the embryo. This often raises more questions than answers. The original cells arising from the meeting of a sperm and ovule are called stem cells or mesen-chyme. Still dormant in our adult connective tissue, they start to move around in the embryo and specialize into organs. French biologist Alexis Carrel (1873–1944)[4], in his study of chicken embryos, observed the development of stem cells into bone structure. He took the already differentiated bone cells and put them into an area of muscle. The cells underwent a dediffer-entiation to specialize into muscle cells. A kind of plasticity to respond to a local stimulus is inherent in these original cells. A great deal of research money is spent these days to try to awaken the stem cells dormant in our connective tissues.

'It seems that the material adapts itself to the immaterial.'[5]

These immaterial forces are super-sensible in nature—an intelligent activity operates in them. This is the beginning of the psychic phenomenon; organs enter into the realm of some psy-chic activity. Each of our organs is not only reshaping the blood stream by carrying food to the cells and waste away, but each organ gives us a basic imprint for our psychic life.

'We must know that, in spite of the fact that they are not fully impregnated with conscious life, all the organs contain the source of the surge directing us towards the psychic life.'[6]

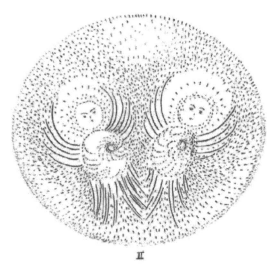

Drawing of the Constellation of Gemini (Twins)

Content

This text explores the imprint of the intelligent activity of Gemini's presence all around us in the constant formation of humans and animals. What is the link between the Gemini sector of space, its glyph, the medieval image of this constellation, Imma's drawing, the element sulphur, the animal phylum Coelenterata, the sense of the ego of another person, the shoulders, Mercury as a ruling planet, the colour yellow and the consonant H? Based on Imma von Eckardstein's drawings, published in the first edition of *The Calendar of the Soul* in 1912, we can try to find a golden thread linking the various ways Gemini acts as a blueprint in nature.

The Glyph and the Traditional Picture

This glyph is often formed by two horizontal curved lines separated by two vertical pillars. The lines above and below can represent sections of two spheres of activity: heavenly and terrestrial, whereas the vertical ones link these two worlds with an impulse inviting symmetry. Radial symmetry developing towards bilateral symmetry is one of the twelve common denominators of living creatures.

The medieval picture of Gemini shows also the mirror images of twins with slight differences. It is two human shapes facing one another. The reason we recognize ourselves in a mirror is that we are built with this bilateral organization. Our image in the mirror is not identical to us — if I close my left eye the image will close its right eye. When things don't have this symmetry they are difficult to recognize. Just try to read writing reflected in a mirror.

Description of the Drawing

The general background of the two creatures here is quite light and made of small lines and points that move towards the periphery in the lower part, suggesting a sphere more than just a circle. At the top there is a greater opening of light.

These two puppet-like drawings have a strong egg-shaped centre with whirling activity in them. The internal lines of force certainly suggest an egg-shaped volume. They express a rhythm of some sort with a vortical tendency. Life manifests always with a germinal cell that expresses itself from inside out. We have here an enclosure or a lighted porous urn (Cancer impulse), but this time with the Gemini impulse these centres want to explode outside. The drawing shows outside line movements at the shoulder level and others at the bottom, both prefiguring future limbs. Two disconnected heads sit above these explosive movements surrounding the active centres.

The two slightly asymmetric beings mirror one another and each of them has bilateral symmetry. These mirror images are not looking at each other, like Narcissus looking at his reflection in a pool of water but are looking outward in the space of the world. We are conscious of spatial direction right and left, front and behind, up and down because of the symmetrical way we are formed.

Sulphur: a Fiery Element

With Gemini we step into the pluricellular animal venture. In the drawing what the central cavity emits reminds us of the fiery nature of sulphur, as when we crack the sulphuric tips of a match to light a candle. Sulphur is a manifestation of Gemini in matter and one of the most reactive substances in chemistry. Where do we find sulphur inside us? Sulphur's affinity for heat and proteins is proverbial and acts like a sculptor. It is an integral part of many proteins. All fermented proteins emanate this sulphuric rotten-egg smell. It shows even in our way of eating: food rich in protein is by tradition prepared with a condiment rich in sulphur, like garlic or mustard.

'Sulphur is seen here as a unifying force that prompts cosmic

essences to work together to build up organic matter in a colloidal stage' (meaning something between solid and liquid, like
jelly).[7] With the animals we are entering into the realm of protein
architecture. Each species has the power to create its own.

'Sulphur is a mediator between the formative forces of the
spiritual and the physical world.'[8]

'The spiritual building forces (and beings) use sulphur as a
sculptor uses water to wet his fingers before kneading the moist
clay into form.'[9]

Sulphur doesn't act in any clear direction; rather it forms
combinations in a social way and creates new possibilities, acting
towards other substances as a cook. Sulphur's function in proteins is just this: it has an affinity for the colloidal stage and thus
for everything alive. It makes the perfect mixer of organic substances. We have here a sculptor that organizes living creative
activities in space.[10]

'Sulphur is very active in the area of an organism where circulation and breathing are close to one another.'[11]

The simplest Pluricellular Animals: from Sponge to Coelenterata

Sponges: 15,000 Species

After unicellular animals we observe the first loosely organized
pluricellular organisms. This is the beginning of a visible protein
architecture. One of the simplest forms of pluricellulars are
sponges that tend to be fixed and look more like plants with
wonderful colours and forms. If we dismantle them without
damaging their cells they will reconstruct their original forms as
if complex lines of force (morphic fields) direct these cells to the
right place. For movement these cells use flagella, cilia,
pseudopods, or simply crystallized silica, calcium or spongin (a
tough type of protein) for rigidity but the whole is a new orderly
'ensemble' under the governance of an new inner architect. It is a
double-walled cavity with a kind of jelly in between.

These animals embrace a much bigger area of the ocean and generate very ingenious compartments to enlarge their contact surfaces with the seawater. This will be an ongoing quest in future phyla, in order to increase and harmonize breathing and circulation. Some of these complex cavities in sponges resemble the alveolar structure of our own lungs.

The More Complex Cavity Animals or Coelenterata

Medusae, Jellyfish, Coral, Hydra, Medusa: 10,000 Species

These simple multicellular animals are embryonic expressions that stop developing beyond the gastrula phase — the embryonic phase where the skin (ectoderm) invaginates or turns inside to create an internal skin (endoderm) generating an inner cavity (gastrula), a cup or an umbrella shape. Here we have the creation of a mirror image: an external skin facing outside, very sensitive and an internal skin facing inside for metabolic functions. Later when we study the two disconnected heads of the Gemini drawing we will meet this dual inner and outer activity.

Inbetween we have a kind of jelly-like substance (mesoglea), a matrix that has free-moving amoeboid cells (collenchyma), secreting calcium, silica (coral) or spongin (hard structural protein), giving different levels of rigidity. It is in this jelly in some species that we find more developed immune and neurological functions.

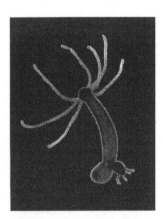

Figs. 1 and 1a represent typical hydra (1a is Haeckel's drawings)

With this involuted skin one orifice forms a kind of mouth-anus. These are the hollow cavity animals — such as medusa, anemone, hydra, coral and jellyfish. In their impulse to come out of the centre some extend upward tentacles like hydra. The upper part of the drawing is eloquent in this

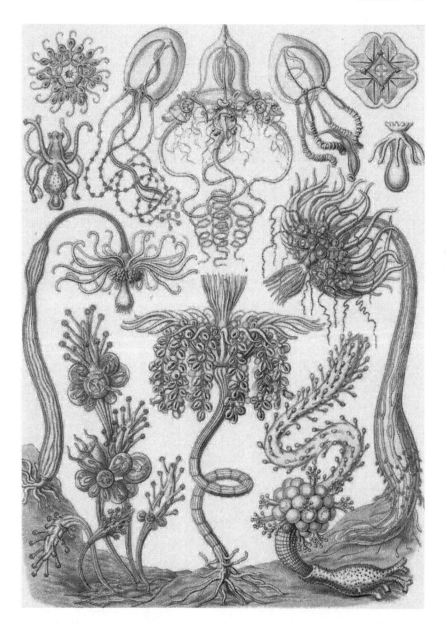

expression (Figs. 1 and 1a). On the other hand, jellyfish (Figs. 2 and 2a) develop downward tentacles. This is expressed at the bottom part of the Imma's drawing. In spite of their soft appearance they sting like nettles with a paralyzing substance.

It is worth mentioning that jellyfish are now on the increase in

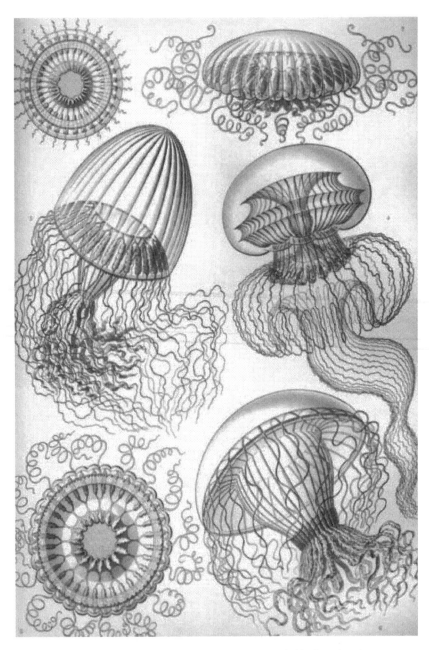

Figs. 2 and 2a represent jellyfishes (Haeckel's drawings)

Fig. 2a

the oceans. They tend to clog fishermen's nets. Is it because, through overfishing, they lose their natural predators or our polluted oceans tend to excite their reproduction?

More complex jellyfish such as the Portuguese man-of-war travel in association with one another forming vast floating

Fig. 3 Drawing of a Portuguese man-of-war or a colony of medusae

ensembles or blooms, each one developing new functions such as a sail above the water surface so that the wind can carry them. Each medusa starts to specialize inside the whole (Fig. 3).

The mirror embryonic membranes that create inner complex cavities can be reversed in the hydra so that what was the digestive inside changes into a neurological outside and vice versa. Again the location determines the function.

It is with some of the phylum Coelenterata that we start the great venture of linking perception (sense organs) with movement (muscles). This drive to develop neural connections allows a nerve apparatus where consciousness can be inside a living being. We might even venture to say that the conscious presence (spirit) of these animal species initiates the neural apparatus for them to be 'in' nature. This is the beginning of an autonomic nervous system leading later in other phyla to more complex brain formation.

'This super-sensible vehicle is a character-bestowing field allowing the animal to experience the environment more than by just being embedded in it.'[12]

'The astral body (soul) welds the shape into an inseparable unity with the behaviour.'[12]

'The outer form is always the final result of these super-sensible systems of forces. So the material adapts itself to the spiritual.'[13]

In each of these egg-shaped centres in the Gemini drawing we observe a nucleus-like activity that tends to gyrate anticlockwise from the centre to the periphery. Be it a seed, egg or bud these germinal cells are a point of anchorage for a spirit to emerge in matter from inside out. The vortex lines of movement start from the centre of the nucleus towards the periphery (anticlockwise or levogyre) rounding up the whole in a spherical shape. There is a mystery hidden in this anticlockwise movement: a climbing plant will always whirl around its support in an anticlockwise gesture.

Other members of this group are fixed such as coral (Fig. 4) and secrete a hard calcium structure. Their expressions in forms and colours create fantastic sub-marine gardens.

Fig. 4 Coral, drawings by Ernst Haeckel

Coelenterata, in their development, often go from the polyp stage where tentacles are up to the medusa stage where the tentacles are down. Some stay at the polyp stage, are fixed and resemble the plant expression. Sometimes they oscillate between the polyp and the medusa stage. Some others live mainly at the medusa stage.

The Molecular Dissymmetry

At a molecular level we find these mirror images too. Atoms in a molecule can be symmetric or asymmetric. The majority of molecules in mineral chemistry have a symmetric image in a mirror, but in organic chemistry the molecules are always dissymmetric. This is demonstrable in a lab by letting a ray of light go through a solution of organic proteins coming from a living creature. The light always gyrates to the left (levogyre).

When a chemist makes a protein in a laboratory, the result is always an equal mixture of both optic forms — half dextrogyre and half levogyre. The isolated dextrogyre protein will gyrate the light towards the right. So half of the proteins made in a laboratory will have the levogyre result, as it is like inside us, and half will have a dextrogyre result which does not occur naturally inside living creatures.

'The unsolved problem is the fact that inside living creatures the proteins and their 20 amino acids are only left-handed (levogyre), whereas genetic material with their 4 nucleotides basis are coiled only as a right-handed (dextrogyre) helix. However, the forces that hold molecules together make no distinction between left and right. No law of nature forbids a left-handed DNA molecule or a right-handed protein or amino acid in living beings. Yet nobody has found one.'[14] This is a simple fact of observation.

'These simple facts are in complete opposition with the laws of physics and the actual model of evolution at random proposed in *Le Hasard et la Nécessité* by French biochemist J. Monod. Is it just an accident? Completely absent in inanimate nature, molecular asymmetry is a unsolved mystery. Living creatures never make dextrogyre proteins. This is a great characteristic aspect of living creatures.'[15]

Be it L-dopa as a remedy or L-tryptophan as a food supplement, pharmaceutical companies, when they sell these products, are quite aware that they must sell a levogyre substance for better assimilation.

The sun, source of light, warmth and life, goes anticlockwise through the zodiac over a period of 25,920 years (called a Platonic year). We are now at the end of the Pisces period and entering soon into the Aquarian period. Does it have something to do with the levogyre aspect of inner organic molecules or the anticlockwise climbing gesture of a morning glory? It is one of the multiple rhythms we are imbedded in. Living creatures are a material manifestation of life that is essentially rhythm.

The Sense of the Ego of Another Human Being

'Sulphur made the Earth a bearer of thoughts that devours life.'[16]

The hollow jellyfish develops the beginning of a central nervous system where sensorial impressions connect with muscles that allow them to move, based on perception. This is the beginning of consciousness in space/time opening the future possibility for a more conscious ego activity in human beings. We have to acknowledge our own ego in order to perceive the ego of another human being. The first step for these organ-animals (jellyfish) is to build a kind of autonomic nervous system with multiple little brains (ganglions). Our whole internal environment is still ruled that way and works below the conscious level (sympathetic and parasympathetic systems).

'Sulphur unites antimony with other metals and also creates a bridge which enables antimony to act on the protein process. The human being is antimony. Antimony processes introduced into the human organization act in the same way as the human ego organization.'[17]

This quote shows us another reason why Steiner attributed the sense of the ego of another human being to the Gemini area of the Milky Way. Antimony is acting in us more as an activity that reflects how the ego intervenes in the building of its own pro-teinic form. This is vital for the perception of the ego of another.

There would be no inward capacity of thinking without this protein architecture. We need sleep because we have exhausted something in our physical construct through the use of our soul faculties that actually devours life. After a good night's sleep we feel refreshed, ready again to think, feel and will in the world. Another reason we sleep is that our ego needs to stay in touch with its spiritual origin — every night we need to go 'home'.

Which brings us to the two heads in the drawing disconnected from their pulsating trunk. They have lateral bisymmetry but they are not quite a mirror image. On the left side the head is smaller, more contracted, with an expression that seems to scrutinize the outside world, denoting the left, more logical, brain. Whereas the right head is bigger and has a more dreamy look representing the more intuitive right hemisphere looking inside. These two heads show the bilateral symmetry the evo-lutionary process is orienting itself towards, still rudimentary in the Coelenterata phylum. Our brain has perfected this tendency with its two hemispheres. We have two worlds here: one is outside perceived through sensory perceptions; the other is the psychic world created inside as a reflection of the outside. Each individual has his own inner mobile psychic landscape that has a continuity with what we perceive outside. These are not two separate worlds but a continuum.

An Urge to Grasp the World: Shoulders-Arms

Out of these central cavities in the drawing something is emer-ging that prefigures the future limb expression. These explosions of possibility, mirroring each other in a bilateral symmetry, can be seen as future wings, fins, limbs, and manifest at the beginning of the simplest pluricellulars. In sponges and hollow creatures (like hydra, jellyfish and coral) we can already observe this tendency. From the hydra to the medusa phase, they emanate tentacles wanting to grasp the world[18] and move around. This is a typical Gemini tendency in the organic world. The tendency to come out of a centre indicates a will to move and grasp that will lead in the future to the embryonic budding shoulders of more evolved phyla. The explosive expression at the shoulder level of the drawing is obvious in the hydra tentacles. On the other hand what is coming out of the dangling bottom part of the drawing is well seen in the pulsing umbrella or bell shape of the jellyfish where their tentacles capture prey. The whole creature looks like a pulsing diaphragm muscle.

In spite of their fragile nature jellyfish are very poisonous with their stinging cells (nematocysts).

Mercury Sphere Rules Gemini

With these first simple pluricellular creatures the importance of cell cohesion is essential. In all of the Coelenterata species a spirit manifests its morphic field or lines of force. This is where the influence of Mercury is at its best, where cells congregate towards a new manifestation.

The metabolic process associated with Mercury is the emergence and maintenance of the material structures of the living body. This process relates to cell and tissue cohesion achieved by fibres holding them together and intercellular messenger activities (hormones acting in a biofeedback loop). All repair, scarring and healing belong here.[19] This maintenance process was essential at the beginning of a collectivity of cells.

'It is Mercury that introduces the substance into the various organs'[20] according to their specific lines of forces (morphic field).

The ancient Greeks saw Mercury as the messenger of the gods. Its function in the organic world is cohesion and mobility of internal systems. This drawing has organized movements in the central figures and also around them. There is only one thing that Mercury will never give up: movement. The god of doctors, thieves, merchants, and jesters (*le fou du roi*), it indicates that this force doesn't allow rigidity. It keeps the 'goods' in circulation. In the intelligent activity of Mercury there is always a certain element of mischievousness—Mercury doesn't allow stagnation or clutter.

The Consonant H

The consonant H is associated with Gemini. This sound expels the air from the lungs by contraction of the abdominal and intercostal muscles, and the breath travels freely through without any tension in the throat or mouth.

'It is a sheet of flame which rises upward or the flare of a flame when a match is struck, the sound of ecstasy.'[21]

There is in Imma's picture a desire to explode towards the outside. It is like an impulse to handle the world. We are not only bubbles in space but we develop extensions to our body. In the drawing the central pulsating trunk wants to exercise outward mobility and grasp the world.

Conclusion

With Gemini we have the impulse to come out of a centre and expand in space in order to grasp the world. This expansion will be a dual organic expression in a radial format then going towards a bilateral format. With Coelenterata it manifests as tentacles of all kinds prefiguring the future fins, wings or limbs of the more complex animals. Their radial symmetry expands in space using mainly six or eight prolongations.

With a dualism, characteristic of the Coelenterata, the two types of Polyp and Medusa are produced. The fixed mode of life of the Polyp leads towards plant life, vegetative growth and solidification. The other path, the Medusa, leads to mobility, to soft and pliable tissues, to sexual differentiation and a more animal-like condition. So we find dualism appearing in the anatomical structure, in the ectoderm and endoderm, in the nervous and digestive systems, and the polarity of the Polyps and the Medusa, and in the division of the species into fixed colonies of the Coral type and the floating colonies of Medusae.[22]

Observing these first pluricellular animals we are struck by the fact that they are made of cell structures similar to the one-cell animals (Protozoa) with their pseudopods, cilia, flagella and capacity to build rigid structures with the silica and calcium found in seawater. We will find them in all animal phyla.

The difference is that it is a new orderly 'ensemble' under the rule of lines of force organizing a new structure based on the previous Protozoa prototypes.

Tens of thousands of new species emerged and are still active today as living organs clarifying the sea. These creatures express an embryonic phase that doesn't go further than forming complex cavities (gastrulation). It seems that here we have an intelligence of some sort or entity (spirit) that can direct the cellular level to a new structural expression with a self-drive to assert itself in matter.

These fleshy organ vessels, umbrellas (jellyfish), are well equipped with their tentacles and venom to paralyze their victims and protect themselves. They are the first protein 'ensemble' in this great adventure of animal expression where sulphur plays a major role. Their contribution in the sedimentation of calcium and silica is enormous, forming islands and mountain ranges. With them we observe a timid start of consciousness 'in' nature where neural connections link perceptions with muscular activities.

At a psychic level the dual symmetry of the brain opens us to inner and outer perceptions. Our civilization tends to feed its thinking life mainly with outer perceptions. The possibility of insights is always there if we listen. Outer perception is in touch with the things surrounding us. Inner perception opens us to the Beings of Things. This needs another methodology which is what the Goethean approach is all about.

The two heads in Imma's drawing reflect this, going from analytical outward listening to a more contemplative inward listening. The thinking process should be fed by outer and inner perceptions. Many scientists in their autobiography talk of important moments of insight in their career. People say 'Oh, he is a genius to have thought of that.' But the fact is—if we allow enough silence to find something, solve a problem, then the 'muse' has a chance to express itself in our consciousness.

3. Taurus

Preamble

For millennia mankind had experienced the earth as an immobile body in space where everything else turned around it (geocentric point of view). In all the light-filled bodies in the night sky they could sense a gigantic dynamic clock impacting on their daily life and psychic abilities.

Then came the Renaissance and through the work of a new wave of astronomers including Nicolaus Copernicus (1473–1543) from Poland, Johannes Kepler (1571–1630) from Germany and the Italian Galileo Galilei (1564–1642) another view was introduced where the planets have an elliptical pathway around the sun – the heliocentric point of view.

After centuries of ever more accurate observations using telescopes and mathematical tools, astronomers succeeded to bring this new view to the fore in spite of religious dogma. The truth is not that one is true and the other one is false. They are both true. It just depends on where we stand. If we play the observer being outside the experience then the heliocentric point of view is a fantastic achievement of the human intellect. If the observer is part of the experience then what he perceives from the earth is a loopy dance of planets making spherical movements around the earth over several years.

We should not really think of the solar system as a precise celestial mechanic but more of a dynamic system where whatever calculation of movement we produce, it must always relate to the mathematical concept of infinity. That is why we have to add one more day every four years (leap years) to catch up with this dynamism, not to mention the odd leap second.

Today with advances in astronomy we have a map of the cosmos that has no stars but just frequencies from radio to gamma rays as well as the enigmatic cosmic rays. Everything is on the move and we are not sure at all if there is a centre. There are areas of heat into the millions of degrees, and others where a thimble of matter weighs ten tons. In our search for the infinitely small (most recently exemplified by the Large Hadron Collider experiments on the French-Swiss border) and the infinity of cosmic space we can only gaze in wonder at Creation and speculate.

Meanwhile we are living on earth inside rhythms of days and seasons due to the Earth's movements in the solar system. All the planets are on the same plane of this elliptical pathway around the sun. When we project this plane into space we arrive at the Milky Way which is our observation of the disc of our galaxy as well as its galactic centre which is estimated to be 28,000 light years in the direction of Sagittarius.

This band across the plane of our galaxy is the home of the twelve constellations we are studying. Nested in this grandiose formation we can ask: What kinds of influence do these constellations and planets send to earth besides electro-magnetic radiations?

Many of Steiner's indications help us think outside the materialistic box that focuses mainly on the sub-sensible world of forces: electricity, magnetism, gravity and the weak and strong forces holding the particles of atoms. Through the mystery of the progressive emergence of living creatures on earth, we can start to open ourselves to other types of forces, supra-earthly and formative in essence. Through the constant recreation of nature and our own human body we can sense that these influences are raining down on us all the time. We can look in the past to guess when and how Creation started, but it is useful to realize that Creation also happens in the 'now' of our present life all the time.

'I perceive the limitless firmament with its worlds floating in space, and the brilliant stars and the suns and moons. And the planets and the fixed stars, and all the contending and reconciled forces of attraction do I see, created and borne by the Will, timeless and without limit. Submitting to a Universal Law whose beginning has no beginning and whose end is without end.'[1]

ꙮ

The Constellation of Taurus (The Bull)

Content

This text explores the imprint of the intelligent activity of Taurus all around us in the constant forming of human and animal creation. What is the relation between the Taurus sector of space, its glyph, the medieval image of this constellation, Imma's drawing, the element nitrogen, the animal phylum echinoderm, the speech/word sense, the larynx, Venus as a ruling planet, the colour orange and the consonant R? Based on Imma von Eckardstein's drawings published in the first edition of *The Calendar of the Soul* in 1912, we can try to find a golden thread linking these various ways Taurus acts as a constant blueprint in nature.

Description of the Glyph and the Traditional Picture

The Taurus glyph is a circle or sphere with two horn-like curves above. In geometry the formula to describe the outline of a horn is similar to the curve of an egg, a bud or a vortex (hyperbole). This formula requires the use of the mathematical concept of infinity.

Horns act as a kind of aerial, grasping subtle influences from the periphery or emitting signals between the various realms. In our sub-world of electromagnetism form and frequency are an indispensable pair. To capture radio or TV frequencies different forms of aerial or antenna are required. Animals have also developed antenna for their own use. There are so many species of insects and each species bears a specific form/aerial tuned to the vast infrared spectrum[2]. We constantly receive multiple and subtle influences from all directions of the cosmos in spite of earth being a little speck of dust as they say in astronomy.

Pictures of the zodiac are not portraits of physical objects, animals or humans. They depict processes, activities of formative forces. The traditional picture for Taurus is a bull. There is a good deal of ferocious movement in there. We have, in the traditional representation of the bull, a clear image of universal, 'all-inclusive force of movement'.[3]

Description of the Drawing

We are in touch here with a vigorous drawing. In none of Imma's twelve zodiac drawings is movement as much emphasized as it is in the Taurus drawing.

This circular drawing has an unusual central form surrounded by a dark and light area becoming lighter at the edge. The outward limit of the circle is porous. Two dark and two light spiral, horn-like movements link the periphery with a centre. Or could it be the opposite: the central figure is raying out towards the periphery? Or maybe it is a dialogue between both—the dark horn moving in and the light one moving out, like a circulatory process.

The central creature is oblique in the drawing, and at its two extremities the two dark and two light vortical movements follow one another. Whether they start at the two ends of this strange creature or arrive there from the periphery is open to question.

Is it a bee of some sort, or larva buzzing around with its eight extensions in the centre of this drawing? One thing is sure: this mobile creature has a dark oval centre well enclosed (CANCER impulse) producing four pairs of clear oval lobes organized in a bilateral symmetry (GEMINI impulse). These eight lobes seem to be mobile with their cilia contours parting the darkness around.

Nitrogen: an Explosive Element

There is only one element that matches the fury of motion of this drawing: nitrogen. We make explosives out of it (nitroglycerine, trinitrotoluene or TNT etc...). What is an explosive if it isn't 'imprisoned motion'?[4] Making up 80 per cent of the air we breathe in its neutral form, nitrogen oscillates between us and the world with oxygen, carbon dioxide, water and various other influences. Nitrogen is not so much part of a chemical compound in nature but has a freer status. In the organic world it is the opposite: it initiates movement.

Steiner saw nitrogen as a manifestation of Taurus in the mineral kingdom. He wrote in his Notebooks 'nitrogen made the earth a spiritualized planet that can adopt the animal form'[5]. Nitrogen has a big role to play: only a protein architecture allows sentient moving beings with specific instinctual behaviours to enter into incarnation.

The architecture of the plant kingdom is carbohydrate, which means that the main elements are carbon, hydrogen and oxygen. If we add nitrogen to these three elements we have proteins that are the main components of animal architecture. Without protein there is no force of motion in animals. Plants produce proteins at the level of their cells and especially in the flower-seed area, but don't take hold of them for external movement. It seems that there is no limit for the expression of proteins in living kingdoms.

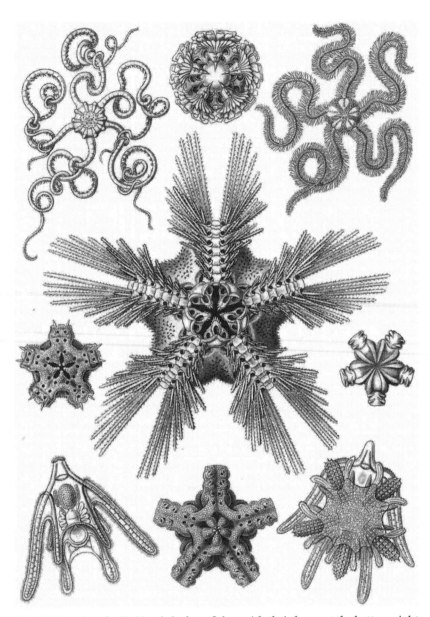

Fig. 1 Drawings by E. Haeckel of starfishes with their larva at the bottom right and left

The Hearing Mouth-Finger: Echinoderm

Starfish, Sea Cucumber, Sea Lilies, Sea Urchin:
3,900 species

If we look at the larva of the echinoderm phylum we find more or less an organization like the one at the centre of Imma's representation of Taurus (in Fig. 1 the bottom left and right images are the larva). The intention here is not only to initiate mobility in order to grasp the world but to hear and see the world.

'No longer merely an enclosing of the Universe but a gaze into its circumference and an apprehension of its mobility.'[6]

The group of animals attributed to Taurus and explored by Kolisko is called echinoderm, such as prickly-skinned animals like the starfish (Fig. 1). Imma's drawing is mainly made of small lines which also makes it seem very prickly. If we look at the larva we find them to be very mobile (full of cilia) free swimmers. In the drawing we can imagine the cilia of the eight lobes parting the darkness. Some of these larvae, such as Dipleurula or Auricularia (bipinnaria), become sinuous and lobed, thus resembling a human ear (Fig. 2). At some other stages of their development these larvae can approach the form of a human larynx with its multiple arms, such as Pluteus. If Coelenterata (medusa or jellyfish) stop at the gastrula level of embryonic development the larvae of this new phylum go a step further with the development of the mesoderm with its free-moving cells that generate more complex organ systems.

It reminds us of the description Steiner gave of the 'swimming-hovering shape with four legs of man's early (Lemurian) ancestors' (H. Poppelbaum, *A New Zoology*).

It is from these elementary larvae that zoologists today work with the hypothesis that the chordates (animals with a vertebral column) emerge

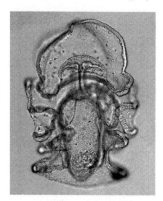

Fig. 2 Photo of Auricularia (meaning 'like ear') larva

through metamorphosis from the hypothetical dipleurula larva of all echinoderms.

Imma's image of Taurus also resembles the pupa of many species of butterflies. The pupa is the mysterious phase between caterpillar and butterfly, allowing metamorphosis. Steiner mentioned that the human larynx with its complex cartilaginous structure is still at an embryonic stage in human development.

The behaviour of our primeval embryonic mesoderm tissue is quite special because the cells in this middle layer are highly mobile and appear to obey morphic fields—areas of space with lines of forces organizing cells and organic substances. The way these original cells generate organs into animal form is all the time an orderly mysterious cavalcade.

Metamorphosis is what is predominant in this phylum. Each starfish begins as a transparent larva and goes through a radical, often colourful, transformation. From radial to bilateral symmetry of the early stage, these larvae, when adults, become pentagonal with five equal sides. A lot of them have a multiple of five fingers (five or ten) while others are spherical such as sea urchins or elongated such as sea cucumber and sea lilies (Fig. 3) but still pentagonal (five).

Part of the middle skin (mesoderm) of these larvae, at one point begins to sprout and imprints the five-ray architecture internally and externally, destroying the rest of the larvae. Most organ systems are present in each of the five sections including the beginning of a nervous system more elaborate than that of the jellyfish. This makes the echinoderm a mesoderm expression, whereas the Coelenterata (jellyfish) was an ectoderm/endoderm manifestation with a kind of amoeboid gelatine in between these two layers. There is no pentagonal symmetry in the crystals of the mineral kingdom. In the plant kingdom, the Rosaceae (apples and pears) are a good example of pentagonal organization. Only the echinoderm in the animal kingdom will express this pentagonal symmetry as a whole creature.

The starfishes do have a dim sense of hearing connected all the time with the seawater passing through them, and also sight—on

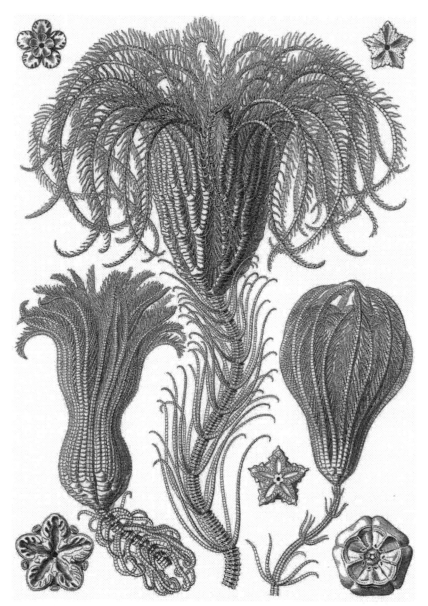

Fig. 3 Drawings by E. Haeckel of sea lilies related to sea urchins and starfishes

the hand of each arm they have primitive eyes. For an organism with hardly any muscles, and with an internal tubular lime structure, the starfish maintains an extraordinary flexibility and really masters an inner and outer mobility. Indeed it is strong enough with the suckers of its fingers to open a bivalve (oyster) and eat the contents.

Circulation, locomotion and breathing work together in one system (ambulacral system), initiating a rhythmic pulse between the ocean (their blood serum) and their internal pliable lime structure.

Their motion is always connected with desires grafted with specific instinctual behaviours. They have a craving for food, air, warmth, protection and an attraction to their polar opposite (sexuality). Through the building of organs grafted with a primitive brain linking perception with movement, a world of feeling and desire can emerge.

'The body as a whole, not merely the nervous activity impounded in it, is the physical basis of psychic life. And just as, for ordinary consciousness, psychic life is naturally classified in terms of ideation, feeling and willing, so is physical life classifiable in terms of neural function, rhythmic occurrence and metabolic process.'[7]

SPEECH or WORD SENSE

In this phylum we have a creature that opens itself to the sound of the sea. Sound travels four times faster in water than in the air and the ocean has more sound than we usually think. In the last 100 years the sound in the ocean has increased at a fantastic rate because of navigation and the use of water by the military to transmit telecommunication frequencies. Its detrimental effect is especially noticeable on animals using ultrasound to communicate (sea mammals like dolphins and whales).

With our ears we can hear sounds but also speech. Words have a structural aspect (consonants) as well as a feeling aspect (vowels). The ability to hear consonants (constellations) and vowels (planets) brings us in touch with an aspect of the Beings of these formative forces.

The animal larynx, like the one in birds and mammals, can

emit all sorts of sounds, usually with emotional signalling content. The human larynx can make sound but also utter structured words. For speech production Broca's area in the left frontal lobe of the brain is especially important.

EAR and LARYNX

Imma's Taurus drawing has a strong relation between centre and periphery. As an example of the relationship between these two we can choose the ear and the larynx. What our ear and brain catch as sounds are waves from the periphery travelling to our internal centre. What the brain and larynx emit are also sound or waves starting from a centre reaching out to the periphery. These organs work together. What is the use of a larynx without an ear? We can't sing a frequency that we can't hear. That is why opera singers tend to observe a decrease in the richness of their voices when they get old and deaf. French scientist Alfred Tomatis (1920–2001) did a lot of research at this level. If a child, in the first two or three years, doesn't hear human language then it seriously impairs his or her future capacity to speak. As we mentioned earlier these two organs have a connection with the centre of this drawing.

> The whole canal system of each foot of the starfish is reminiscent of a seemingly far remote structure, namely the labyrinth in the inner ear of the vertebrate. The five canals can be compared with the three semi-circular canals of the ear, and the stone (lime) canal with the endolymphatic duct of the human ear. It cannot be mere chance that the whole phylum of the Echinoderm bears such a resemblance (lymph flowing in calcareous bone) to an auditory organ.[8]

From our larynx/naso-pharynx two tubes (Eustachian tubes) reach up into the middle ear. First we need the equipment to hear words (ears) and then we need the organ to produce them (larynx). It is astonishing to find similar structures in the embryonic aspect of this phylum.

Fig. 4 A representation of Venus, five loops around the earth over a period of eight years (see Note 10)

Venus Sphere Rules Taurus

The planet Venus makes five loops around the earth over a period of eight years (Fig. 4). This is from a geocentric point of view which means that if you have the patience to observe over eight years the movement of Venus you will notice these five loops. The reason why we have these loops for all the planets is because the earth is not static and moves also inside the solar system.

As we have seen, the echinoderms are the only phylum using mainly five or ten as their whole radial structure. The Venus metabolic process has to do with harmonious growth and regeneration helping the constant renewal of our organs. It is an energizing force coupling beauty of proportion and flamboyant colours with movement. This harmonizing activity is important here because many more organ systems emerge in these creatures. The internal liquid has active amoeboid stem cells giving this phylum its amazing capacity for regeneration.

The metal associated with Venus is copper. Like all metals, it is a congealed flowing force. It is colourful in both the mineral and the living realm, and used with profusion by this phylum and other phyla. It is also an essential micro element (enzymatic co-factor) for the efficient use of the B vitamin group (another enzymatic co-factor) which activates the growing process.

CONSONANT R

As for the consonant attributed to Taurus we just have to remember the 'rrrrowing' sound of the bull. 'It is more a rolling sound than a consonant from the larynx', said Steiner. 'It is especially true with the guttural "Rrrr", freeing our tongue (the bud of the heart), thereby our soul, from the weight of the physical body. Unhappily in the English language, this sound is rarely given its full pronunciation.'[9]

Conclusion

Taurus initiates an instrument that can see and hear its surrounding and move accordingly in spite of its internal lime structure. A periphery and a centre relate strongly in Imma's drawing. This is what the echinoderm are constantly doing: harmonizing pulsing seawater in and out within a rigid lime structure.

A roaring bull stands and suddenly rushes forwards—all its power is between its head and body, mainly its neck and larynx. With a more complex nervous system than the Coelenterata, the echinoderm ensoul more the feeling and willing aspect of their soul. The internal motion harmonizes with the external world.

In their embryonic phase they are part of the plankton of the ocean. Their adult forms are numerous and they all use the seawater as their internal blood serum. Movement, circulation and breathing are one.

Influenced by the strong impact of Venus moving around the earth (five loops in eight years),[10] the echinoderm metamorphosis prefigures our own bone organization. We have five regions in the vertebral column, five parts in each limb and five fingers and toes at the end of each limb. All planets dance a loopy choreography around the earth. This is our observation. The ancients knew this mixture of subtle zodiac influences interacting with the planets of the solar system and called it The Music of the Spheres. Wherever 'ballet' there is always a meaningful activity.

4. Aries

Preamble

'For the Verb impregnates the whole cosmos and the formation of the worlds is the preserved expression of the Verb.'[1]

We have spoken of the abundance of frequencies that the cosmos sends us (from radio to x-rays, gamma and other rays). Are the stars sending only these? Through our sense perception man's consciousness has access to a small proportion of what the sensible world emits. Bees can perceive ultraviolet. Predators with senses of smell hundreds of times better than ours track their prey or mates by smell. Animals are aware of an imminent earthquake hours before it happens. In China, a country prone to earthquakes, each province has a call centre where people ring if they observe abnormal animal behaviour. Whales communicate by ultrasound from one ocean to another. We live in an ocean of natural frequencies and the development of telecommunication (the use of frequencies to send information such as radio, television and cellular networks) has increased these a millionfold since the Second World War.

Surrounding us there are specific forces from the infra-earthly realm. Our awareness of an up and down is due to gravity. Babies spend a few years mastering this force with their muscular-skeleton system in order to stand vertically. Out of gravity, in space, astronauts quickly lose bone density.

Unlike gravity, magnetism is more difficult to grasp without an instrument but it is an essential component of the earth's atmosphere. This North-South field that extends far away into space beyond the moon protects us (like a very subtle ozone layer) from the continual bombardment by charged particles from the sun. By trapping most of them towards the North and South Pole it allows life to express itself. The phenomenon of the

Aurora Borealis is connected with this. It is not the subject of this study to look at the multiple skins/layers surrounding the earth but at all the living creatures.

Our awareness of electricity in nature has more to do with lightning and thunder. This force, like the others, is also inside us; we produce a kind of electrical and magnetic activity by using our muscles and brain. We can also heal muscular-skeletal injuries with properly applied electro-magnetic frequencies: this is regularly used in physiotherapy for athletes.

Modern-day technology is based on the mastery of these fundamental forces.

This text focuses on the assumption that there are also supra-earthly forces responsible for the emergence of the various kingdoms of nature and that these forces are still continually raining down on us with the help of our central sun. This aspect will be treated in more detail in the Preamble of Aquarius in Chapter 6.

Because these super-sensible formative powers generate the sensible world, a shadow is produced (the sub-earthly realm). Suppose a light shines on an object producing a shadow, and you

The Drawing of the Constellation of Aries
(The Ram)

perceive only the object and its shadow. That is what science today is studying: the sensible object and its shadow[2]. In this example the light represents the super-sensible forces.

By qualifying the formative powers that come from the stars, this text examines one of the greatest unresolved mysteries in biology: the emergence of species with their intricate forms that constantly renew themselves.

We can call it bio-astronomy. Biodynamic farming, that relies on the constellation and planet positions for the organization of food production, already applies this discipline for the growth of plants, animals and the health of the ecosystem of the farm.

Content

This text explores the imprint of the intelligent activity of Aries' presence all around us in the constant formation of human and animal creation. What is the relation between the Aries sector of space, its glyph, the medieval image of this constellation, Imma's drawing, the element silica, the animal phylum tunicata, the thinking sense, the cranium, Mars as a ruling planet, the colour vermillion and the consonants V and W? Based on Imma von Eckardstein's drawings published in the first edition of *The Calendar of the Soul* in 1912, we can try to find a golden thread linking the various ways Aries acts as a constant blueprint in nature.

Description of the Glyph and the Traditional Picture

Glyphs are symbols of dynamic forces showing the working of the constellation in the kingdoms of nature. The Aries glyph can be seen as two curved lines around the eyes fusing at the nose into one descending line. This force, like all the others, is an impulse to organize matter in a certain way, a vector of activity.

'It is like a lightning action, something which wants to go in a certain direction and bring about movement, evolution.'[3]

If we project this glyph inside we have the vertical spinal cord becoming, on its way up, two brain hemispheres well protected by the three meninges in a bony cranium.

In the cycle of the seasons Aries is positioned with the return of the increase of light and warmth (spring in the northern hemisphere). Because of that Aries is often seen as the first constellation, a new growth period, the beginning of a cycle of time. We can also say that at the beginning of physical evolution there seemed to be an intention to produce a cranium that can hold an apparatus of communication (nervous system) between the physical and the supra-physical. The glyph is made of two parts which could be the tops of two connected spheres. Two worlds connect: the terrestrial and the spiritual. We can also see in this glyph the lightness of a flying bird. That is what thought forms are: they come and go with the levity of birds.

The cranium in this context is a miniature image of the greater cosmos. Both have this vault roundness. In this Aries impulse we have an intention to create a vertebral and cranial container for the development of the future brain, which will be, in the course of evolution, more and more a captor-reflector of cosmic thought forms. This kind of hard bony well-protected vault surrounding the brain allows an enclosed conscious spirit to listen. The human brain in this cranium will take back into itself through the senses what is spread out in the physical universe and 'in as much as one looks back at oneself one finds the universe'.[4] Aries is an initial creative impulse giving us the possibility to perceive the sensible and super-sensible realms manifested as nature.

The traditional picture shows a Ram looking over his shoulder. Its great spiralled horns listening to the world beyond. Looking backwards is, in this context, to be aware of the influences raying down from universal space. The two heads in Imma's drawing, descending in the dense world, look toward the realm where they come from.

It is through the cranial and vertebral sensory doors that the

brain develops especially in early childhood. Without perceptions of the outer world the human mind can't develop, and it
takes several years to master this powerful tool that gathers
ideas, thoughts, concepts, insights and memories and assembles
them into a coherent discourse. We all know, however, how
difficult it is to shut it when we want to put the mind to rest.

The air around us is chock-a-block with images, music,
thought forms that come from various civil and military channels. To capture them we need a radio or TV apparatus: they are
transducers that transfer information from a sub-earthly realm to
the sensible realm of our senses. Nobody will say that the radio
produces the program. It is quite recent in human history to say
that the brain is producing our thoughts. Even in the Middle
Ages scientists and artists might have said: What I am writing are
insights from the supra-earthly realm.

When someone like a scientist is strongly focused there is a
kind of tuning. Insights can take the form of images, sound or
intuition—it is a perception from inside us. We become conscious of these insights because the brain is also a transducer. It
reflects the myriads of thought forms generated by the supra-
earthly realm and also by human beings on earth. But we have to
tune in. How to tune to the 'Beings of Things' will be broached in
the Preamble of the next chapter when we look at methodology.

Description of the Drawing

In Imma's representation of Aries, from the clear left periphery
something is raining down, pushing two human profiles in a
diagonal way towards the right, a realm of more density. It
seems that these heads are floating in space. The first profile is
only an outline of a human face. The second has its full head
with abundant lively hair. Is it a man or a woman? It is a face
with several sense organs. The first one is more ethereal and
the second one has more physical presence, it has a definite
physical head and cranium. As the first zodiac sign, Aries

shows the direction the evolutionary process is going to take. We will see with the animal phylum that the cranium is on its way right at the start of animal evolution. Here we are not in the realm of random mutation but intentional progress — purposeful evolution.

It is through the face that we perceive light, sound, taste, smell. What is the point of a cranium or brain apparatus if there is no perception entering into it? What use are eyes if there is no light to perceive? These sensorial percepts reaching our consciousness are formative not only for our psyche but for the whole body. Sense impressions are also forces.

> Each of the sense organs, it was understood [in the past] is also a force, a soul force, projecting out into the world, meeting there with forces from the object being perceived. Actual perception, understood from this view, consists of the unified field between the perceiver and the perceived. This a kind of imagination that is still necessary to understand what is meant by a perception of the heart. Without this kind of imagination, all that is said concerning the heart falls into mushy sentimentality having no substance and no actuality.[5]

Transference of Information: Silica

Which substance goes through a biological system unaltered and tends to come out at the boundary of organs or organisms? Silica.

Silica is abundant in the earth's crust (c. 45 per cent) associated with many other minerals and as quartz contained in many types and deposits (e.g. clay, sand, granite, etc). In its pure form it is a transparent hexagonal crystal. This six-sided organization is seen in beehives as well as in the microstructure of the liver and bones. Thanks to it, we have glass in our windows. It transfers visual information without distortion. Very useful as 'microchips' in computers — when doped with a bit of arsenic or germanium it becomes a semiconductor and transfers information.

In water it disappears but doesn't dissolve like salt. Silica in the water of our internal liquids, is not in solution but in an inbetween labile stage that can in a twinkling of an eye go over into a solid by way of a gelatinous flaky stage (hydrogel), or can become fully liquefied, turning into a true solution (hydrosol).

Silica inside our body tends towards a colloidal state between liquid and solid, like proteins. It is interesting to note that in human physiology books silica is rarely mentioned. Maybe it is because it has no known structural activity. It tends to go through us and lodge at the periphery of internal membranes like the pleura of the lung or external membranes like the skin with its hair and nails. When burned our body has 7g of silica in its ashes.

'The silica made the earth a copy of the cosmos.'[6]

Silica transfers the subtle supra-earthly influences to living creatures. At the surface of our skin and internal membranes we have a constant very fine silica mantle.

'The colloidal state is characterized chiefly by a considerable increase in surface tension.'[7]

It is denser at its surface. Being denser silica has a more reactive surface for energy transfer. Fleeces and feathers are full of silica. Is this why the shamans and witch doctors used them as garments in special ceremonies – to increase subtle communication with the super-sensible?

The Beginning of a Notochord: Tunicata

Tunicata: c. 2,150 species

With the tunicata we have a first step in evolution towards the chordata. These are animals that have a notochord which is the precursor to our vertebral column. These animals arrive very early in the fossil record. In the tunicata, we have an animal expression that shows this future orientation towards the vertebrate form. The tunicata appears like so many other invertebrates during the 'Cambrian explosion' – a geological period 542 million years ago where suddenly the rock strata hold a huge variety of animal species.

The group of animals called tunicata is the most representative to explain the nature of the Aries formative force in the animal kingdom. If we consider the tunicata (cephalochordata or head-vertebra) in their larval forms, we see the first embryonic attempt to create a head centre (tadpole shape) with the possibility, through their notochord and dorsal tubular nerve cord, of a future vertebral column. Lancelet (amphioxus lanceolatus) for instance, is still a swimming embryo in the ocean today (about six inches long). With its mouth in front and anus at the back it prefigures all future vertebrate animal forms. The biologist Ernst Haeckel at the end of the nineteenth-century called it 'the most noble ancestor of man'. In their free-swimming larval forms they are the sisters of all vertebrates with similar ribosomal DNA. Thousands of species are still active in the oceans today.

The notochord is a flexible cartilaginous rod-like structure of mesodermal cells formed during gastrulation that induces the formation of the neural plate (neurulation), synchronizing the development of the neural tube. Post-embryonic vestiges of the notochord are found in the nucleus pulposus of our cartilaginous inter-vertebral discs.

In this group of animals we notice a striking genome plasticity with possible cross-species gene transfer. They have a high level of vanadium and lithium in their blood and can concentrate heavy metals. Even today this phylum acts as a great cleaner of the ocean and are on the increase. When the larval form becomes adult there is a great morphologic transformation where the pro-chordata characters leave their places to some sort of colourful fixed bag shape called sea squirt.

As humans, we all pass through this larva stage on the way to incarnation by building first a notochord. The tunicata also have the rudiments of all the future organic systems including the neurosecretory cells similar to the master gland — the pituitary — in vertebrates. The basic organization of the vertebrate endocrine system appears very early in these creatures.

Another tunicata is salp. It is the fastest growing pluricellular (Fig. 1). Its larval stage is often organized, with other larvae, like

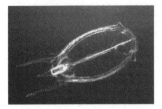

big long tubular worms moving in synchronicity via bioelectric signals.

The Thinking Sense

Fig. 1 Photo of a salp

Words and sentences have meanings that can be grasped because they represent thought forms. With tunicata there is an orientation towards the brain equipment that allows humans to enter into the way another human thinks through his speech or written words.

This sense is not to be confused with our own thinking process.

'The thought—I want to dance—is something of a spiritual nature, even if it's so that the trace of the thought is registered by the brain. The brain and the motor pathways are material. How in the world can the two interact?' The will is involved and it is 'the most unconscious aspect of our being. We hardly know anything about the will...'[8]

Will is this unconscious soul faculty that constructs and maintains us. The conscious mind can use the surplus if it is available. When sick or when we are growing, the availability is restrained. That is why after our growth is finalized this fantastic etheric power of construction can be used for the thinking activity.

'In the brain the smaller sphere appears like a mirror of the greater one. Human thoughts have their origin in Divine Thoughts but they die into a shadowy existence [concept] as soon as they touch the human brain.'[9]

The grasping of concepts at an early age is still a puzzle for linguists. It is a form of clairvoyance that we perform on a daily basis. The intelligence of things talks to us all the time. A special centre in the brain is connected with this capacity to interpret another person's thought forms. Imma's Ram (Aries) drawing shows two heads in profile representing the left side only where the more rational brain resides. It is in the left frontal lobe (Broca's area) that we have the aptitude to produce meaningful sentences (spoken and written), and it is in the higher association centre (the Wernicke's area) of the left temporal lobe that the symbolic meaning of words is understood.

The two heads of the drawing seem to utter words with their mouths slightly open, imitating what is heard from the supra-earthly sphere. Kepler, in his book *Harmony of the Spheres*, looked at the common denominator uniting geometry, music and astronomy.

'He was following Pythagorus's initial insight that in the planetary movement there are correspondences between musical intervals, planetary rhythms and geometric archetypal patterns.'[10]

The music of the spheres refers to this complex rhythmic choreography performed by the planets around the earth. Like any choreography it is an activity that has meaning. John Martineau in his book *A Little Book of Coincidence in the Solar System* is eloquent on this.

'The right hemisphere is actually superior in representational and visual-spatial functions (art), in perception and discrimination of musical tones and speech intonations, in emotional responses, and in understanding humour and metaphors.'[11]

'The left one is more verbal, logical (mathematic), analytical and reducing things to their parts to understand them.'[11]

The right and left hemispheres are in constant dialogue through the corpus callosum if they had the chance in early childhood (during the first four years) to develop their connections properly. Each part of the left hemisphere is connected with the right one. They work in tandem.

An Image of the Roundness of the Cosmos: The Cranium

The drawing emphasizes the head-cranium formation as a small sphere that contains the brain and that reflects the greater cosmic sphere. The brain becomes a captor-reflector not a creator of thoughts. Aries initiates in the tunicata a notochord template, a ruler for the future formation of an enclosed nervous system. Human embryos very early form this cartilaginous notochord.

Mars Sphere Rules Aries

One aspect of Mars' warrior energy is living beats or pulsations. In the internal environment it is also represented in digestive activity: in the bile that helps the dismantlement of food, for instance. It is also a living beat around the brain's grey cells, digesting the impressions from outside. Mars imposes pressure and tension by stretching our internal membrane. In the same way that we have to create tension in a guitar string to get a specific note, our meninges around the brain need tension to tune the grey cells for reception of thoughts.

The sensorial organs capture the outer impression, the nerves preserve it, but to reach our consciousness there must be a pulse around the grey cells. Each breath moves the cerebrospinal fluid that surrounds the grey cells. This mineral fluid is produced and reabsorbed constantly, generating a certain pressure that holds the meninges in tension.

'It is owing to the contact of the breathing-rhythm with the nerve-currents that we can form pictures of the outer world. Abstract thoughts depend still on the nerve-life, but the *pictorial* and *formative* is connected with the breathing [pulse]. We can say: here we have the formative life, and since we breathe we have it in us. It lives naturally in the human form and partakes in it.'[12]

Pictorial — when the percept becomes image-representation in our consciousness, this is the start of our thinking activity and its constant reshuffling.

Formative — when these images or blueprints travel in the body with the sun process (blood circulation). Sense perception doesn't feed only our psychic activity but is also the basis of our bodily form.

> The external human body is formed according to the zodiac (*twelve form elements*), and since this formative life is mediated through the

breath and lives in man's form, it participates too in what is formed externally from the starry heavens. This external formation is thereby co-ordinated as well into man's inner being. And it is due to the breath [pulses] that not only man's conscious breathing is the outcome but that pictures of all the inner organs arise in imitation of the outer form. Thus, in the first place, the inner organs are formed as pictures by way of the breathing processes. They are not yet substantial; the breath [pulse] forms first a picture of the inner man. As we move with the earth in the zodiac [surrounded by the moving planets] we are all the time inhaling the pictures [through sense perception] of our inner organization. We breathe them [impressions] in from the external world.[12]

Another important process associated with Mars is destruction. This is seen in the tunicata in their tendency for metamorphosis — destruction must come first for the new form to emerge.

There are two types of soft-body tunicata without bone structure. One is immobile and called sea squirt with a tunic made of cellulose (this substance belongs more usually to the plants). The other type is called salp and looks like a little fish. Sea squirt in their larval stage all have a notochord that degenerates later (this destruction-digestion of the embryonic phase is also a Mars process). It is a metamorphosis which in its first stage is always destructive (Mars).

The Consonants V and W as an Expression of Aries

The V is made 'by holding the top teeth against the inner edge of the lower lip' whereas in W (ou) 'the lips are contracted into a tight rose shape and released'[13] pushed by the abdominal muscles. Both sounds vibrate like buzzing bees making the lips tremble. As sounds, they are perceived by the soul as living waves.

The mouth, used before to bring food in, lets the warm breath of the lungs invade it to emit sound with emotional content with the help of the belly muscles contracting (metabolic centre).

Warm-blooded animals are good at it. The head, thorax and abdomen are involved in producing sounds. Man started early to produce articulate sounds (vowels and consonants) 'that heralded the start of the penetration of the ego into a human body'.[13]

Conclusion

In the Protozoa (Cancer impulse) we have the beginning of the ectoderm (exterior sensitive skin). With the Coelenterata (Gemini impulse) the endoderm (interior digestive skin) is added to these simplest multicellular creatures. Then with the echinoderm (Taurus impulse) the mesoderm (middle skin) comes into being. This is the successive evolution of the three layers of embryonic tissues.

'In the tunicata these three layers are combined to give the archetype [larva] of all embryological evolution. In this animal group is the secret of the animal that starts to become its individual self. This is why Ernst Haeckel was so occupied with the tunicata in his study of the animal kingdom.'[14]

These creatures bridge the gap between invertebrates and vertebrates. This embryonic formation proves to be the archetypal stage of the higher animal types. We all pass through this stage at the beginning of our venture into incarnation.

This phylum is called tunicata because it secretes a coat of tunicin, a substance almost identical to cellulose which reminds us of how close animals and plants were to one another at the beginning of life on earth. In this phylum, as in the drawing, we have a kind of forerunner of a future prophetic form (the full head of the drawing). Aries initiates a round head that will receive thought forms.

In the present evolutionary process the human head captures the forms of earthly things in order to retain these in consciousness. The head, in higher forms, is a focus for sense perception and assimilation. In this drawing the complete head, descending in the realm of density, looks at the archetypal outline. The traditional Aries picture is a ram turning its head, aware of where it has come from.

It is a matter of fact that the silica we breathe and eat tends to go through us in a colloidal state and sits at the periphery of all membranes (skin, serous membrane, placenta, sense organs). Silica seems to reflect the blueprint of formative forces in a movement from outside in. Coming from all directions of space, these formative forces are constantly captured by the thin layer of silica on the surface of our membranes. Aries-silica gives us the power to receive subtle influences.

'As carrier of life, all fluids in living creatures are colloidal. In our body silica is located where we find internal or external envelopes protecting functional organs.'[7]

By absorbing water, silica becomes a captor of subtle influences lodging in the internal connective tissue lining of nerves, blood vessels, joints, organs or external peripheric growth (skin, hair, feathers, wool).

It is the Mars influence through its breathing pulses around our grey matter that allows the outside impressions to reach our consciousness.

5. Pisces

Preamble

'Compared to the outer splendour and majesty of rivers and mountains, of the earthly world, all that is inside the human skin—as our physical organization—is much greater and more majestic... If you look at one single alveolus it is more magnificent than the mightiest Alpine mountain range. What is inside the human body is a condensation of the entire spiritual cosmos. In the human organization we have an image of the entire cosmos.'[1]

This condensation is also in constant recreation at every second of our life supported by the activity of the states of matter and their etheric counterparts.

English scientist Francis Bacon (who developed an empirical theory of knowledge with a new classification of sciences) said to the scholastic theologians in his *Novum Organum* (1620), in effect:

Stop talking about the world and start to observe things. By doing so you might discover laws and properties of matter that can lead towards scientific advantages for your fellow human beings.

It was a call for modern scientific research. Around the same time René Descartes, the French philosopher, mathematician and physicist, created a methodology in *Discours de la méthode* in 1628.

In science an observer, investigating a phenomenon, directs his thoughts towards it—he observes, hypothesizes and experiments. He stands outside the object and what he discovers is modelled into theories that are constantly amended, as he adds more information to the observed phenomenon. Both Bacon and Descartes wanted to distance themselves from the confusions of medieval scholastic priests.

Then Goethe came and said to scientists: stop looking only at things by fragmenting the physical world and start to look at the

Beings of things, at the intelligent activity behind things. By doing so you let the phenomenon talk to you. It is due to Steiner that we have a better understanding of Goethe's methodology. Steiner was asked to go through Goethe's estate and manuscripts which had been left untouched since his death (1832) — Steiner helped publish and bring attention to Goethe's achievements and methodology.

This method allowed Goethe to make many original scientific discoveries as described in *Plant Metamorphosis* (1790) and the *Theory of Colours* (1810). Here too we have an object of observation and an observer. But this time the observer is integral to the observed phenomenon. In actual fact, it is the activity behind the phenomenon that the observer is going to perceive. Goethean observation is first contemplative, and then intuitive discernment is applied to separate fantasy from real insight. In order to achieve this, another form of intelligence must awaken that connects us more with the heart-feeling than the brain-thinking process.

Soul qualities are needed to open to the intelligent activity in the phenomenon perceived.

First, facing the physical manifestation — be it a plant, a patient or a star system — a feeling of awe and wonder should pervade the soul before the mystery observed.

'In a sense we may say that all knowledge must have wonder for its seed.'

'A thinking that is set in motion without the condition of wonder remains nothing but a mere play of thought.'[2]

Whatever we observe with our sense perceptions there is always a mystery behind it. A plant is not known because we put a name on it and dissect it to its smallest parts. The mystery of form still eludes us.

Second, to penetrate the intelligent activity behind the manifestation, and open a kind of communication, a sense of reverence and veneration must be cultivated for the active forces or Beings who created it. Then we open a door for insight or inner perception.

'Any thinking that is divorced from reverence, that does not behold in a reverent manner what is proffered to its view, will not be able to penetrate to (subtle) reality.'[2]

Third, the soul must let go of separateness. Only the intellect separates us in space and suggests a here and a there. In fact there is no separation — everything is connected. Mere thinking is worthless. In each new discovery of matter's properties, like the double helix of DNA, scientists think they can now comprehend the mystery of forms. This was especially true with the successful sequencing of the human genome which was expected to yield so many answers but mostly generated more questions about genes.

Each discovery increases our ignorance because more questions come to the fore. If we feel ourselves 'in wisdom-filled harmony with the laws of the world'[2] we have more chance to be open to insights. Goethe said:

'We ought really never to make judgements or hypotheses concerning external phenomena; for the phenomena are the theories, they themselves express their ideas, if only we have grown mature enough to receive impressions from the phenomena in the right way.'

'This is what placing oneself in harmony with objects means.'[2]

Fourth, we must 'surrender to the active ruling will and wisdom of the world'.

'We have to learn to adopt a passive attitude (active listener) to the things of the world, and let them speak out their own secrets.'

'We have a wonderful example in Goethe, who, when he wanted to investigate truth, did not allow himself to judge but tried to let the things themselves utter their own secrets.'[2]

In science or art we say a man is a genius who can tap into insights nourishing the thinking and feeling intelligence with inner as well as outer perceptions.

As for the intuitive discernment it 'is more like a spiritual instinct that operates without the intervention of intellect reflection'[3]. It feeds the intellect with inner perception. If the one receiving insights appropriates them as his own, then he or she cuts the communication with the spirit world. By being thankful for the insights we pre-empt the egotistic tendency to possess them and open a channel for more.

As we have to tune a complex piece of technology (radio) to get the right programme that is already there in the air we, with our complex organ-system, can tune to thought forms that are already there around us in more subtle realms.

Both scientific methods (Descartes and Goethe) need to be practised with a strong disciplined will.

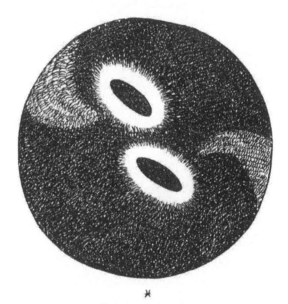

The Drawing of the Constellation of Pisces
(Fishes)

Content

This text explores the imprint of the intelligent activity of Pisces' presence all around us in the constant forming of human and animal creation. What is the relation between the Pisces sector of space, its glyph, the medieval image of this constellation, Imma's drawing, the element chlorine, the animal phylum molluscs, the hearing sense, the feet, Jupiter as a ruling planet, the colour rose and the consonant N? Based on Imma von Eckardstein's drawings published in the first edition of *The Calendar of the Soul* in 1912, we can find a golden thread linking the various ways Pisces acts as a constant blueprint in nature.

Description of the Glyph and the Traditional Picture

The Pisces glyph shows two vertical parallel curved lines. They can be seen as two portions of a circle or spheres of activity attached to one another with a band in the horizontal plane. Some traditional representations show two fishes swimming in opposite directions linked together by a banderole (a light band of tissue) in their mouths.

With the Pisces glyph the spheres stand horizontally. In the Gemini glyph the top sphere stands for the supra-earthly forces descending into the earthly sphere imposing a progressive bilateral symmetry. There are in this glyph two opposite trajectories in a state of cooperation, two sets of activity going in different directions but still connected to one another.

Our psychic waves of images from a past we can't change, and a projection of images into a future we can't predict, have to harmonize in the consciousness of the present moment. Our internal environment constantly goes from dissolution to crystallization where internal rhythms mimic external ones. We live also in a cycle of becoming (in-carnation) and passing away (ex-carnation). We are all aliens on earth, in transit.

As for this last cycle, it is relevant to mention American scientist David Bohm's (1917–1992) ideas of Implicate and Explicate order. As a scientist who contributed to the physics of particles, he stipulated a multidimensional world where the Explicate dimension is the realm of the physical manifestation (the maya concept of the Hindus), whereas the Implicate order is more akin to Greek philosopher Plato's (c. 428–347 BCE) Ideals or archetypes — the realm of the spirit.

The consequence of the above-mentioned orders and their interactions is 'enfolded structures that interweave and interpenetrate each other, throughout the whole space, rather than between the abstracted and separated forms that are manifested to our senses'.[4] For Bohm, there was no real separation between phenomena. They are all influencing each other. It is an illusion to think that the observer cannot influence what he is observing.

'Because consciousness has no substance it can be understood in terms of a dimension that is closer to the Implicate order than the Explicate order... The actual structure, function and activation of thoughts is in the Implicate order.'[4]

> On one hand we need to be able to imagine two orders of existence: earthly and spiritual. On the other hand, we need to imagine these two worlds of existence functioning, not in tandem, but as one, without collapsing the one into the other ... for the normal ego, it has to be one or the other ... but it takes courage to accept that they co-evolve together ... We are able to live in the perceptual experience of the ordinary world while we simultaneously live in the soul experience of the spiritual world.[5]

Believing the earthly world is the only one is materialistic. Believing the spiritual world is the only one is spiritualistic. According to American psychoanalyst Robert Sardello both tendencies are 'neurotic dissociation'. The spiritual and the material co-evolve all the time.

Description of the Drawing

Imma's Pisces drawing has a dark background, sparkled with white dots. Some ancient cultures saw the night sky as a punctured canvas. Through the holes they saw light as stars or planets. With this drawing we touch the dense earth, personified in the past as the Black Madonna—an aspect of Mother Earth—the active listener.

Then, carved out of this dark background, we have two dark oval lumps surrounded by a white halo that part the dark surrounding. These white haloes behave like light irradiating into the dense medium. Or maybe it is the dense matter that wants to penetrate the area of light. Whichever it is, at the edge of the black surrounding and white haloes, there is a balanced activity. The dark ovals can be seen as footprints creating a pressure on the dense earth which irradiates as white haloes. If so, there is an exchange of energy between the owner of the feet and the solid ground.

Put a quartz crystal under pressure and it reacts by emitting a stable signal called piezoelectricity. The same applies to our crystalline bone structure when we walk on earth. This compression stimulates the osteocytes to build more bone deposit. Astronauts spending time out of gravity have to rebuild their muscle-bone structure when they come back.

From the middle of the two dark lumps emerge two vortical grey forms, moving in opposite directions. These funnel-like forms look like scaly vibratory well-structured movements (a bit like a paved pathway), parting the dark aspect of this drawing and increasing in size towards the periphery. The whole organization has an oblique orientation where the periphery is united with these 'ova' (dark lumps) by the funnels.

'These two ova can be seen as two footprints with the ether currents flowing from them.'[6]

One foot shows a movement towards the physical world, and the other tends to go towards the spiritual while still on earth. Whatever direction they take these two footprints stay strongly in touch with solid Mother Earth.

It is obvious in this drawing that the two funnels (vortices) go in different directions. And they start in an area of the foot called in acupuncture 'the spurting out, gushing forth fountain'. This suggests a permanent flow of energy, an energetic dialogue between the rhythms of the earth and those of humans, through the feet. This acupuncture point is the beginning of the kidney meridian. The kidney landscape presides over the manifestation of the human form by harmonizing pure fluidity (diverse moving liquids) with extreme rigidity (mineral bones). The kidneys are the main diluter of our minerals and salts. Most minerals act in us at a highly diluted level as indispensable vectors of activity training enzymes towards the construction of organic substances.

In reflexology the feet, like the ears, represent the totality of the organism. They are a map of our internal make-up.

Chlorine: a Builder of Salt

What is the main internal ground that allows living creatures to build sets of organs? We might say water, but it is more exact to say salty water. We can't escape the fact that all our cells spend a lot of energy maintaining the right concentration of salt, and not only table salt. This concentration in us is similar to the one in the ocean.

In the ocean the balance of salt has been maintained over the aeons. The rivers of the continents pour the salt of the earth into the ocean all the time. Ocean water has succeeded in maintaining its concentration of salt at around 3 to 4 per cent. If it goes above five per cent then life is threatened. One way to control salt content is to deposit it at the edge of the continents (tides) where water can evaporate. Through geological metamorphic processes, many salt deposits created at sea level in the past have been uplifted—e.g. Himalaya salt deposits or buried under the ground as found in salt mines.

'The key element in determining ocean salinity is chlorine.'[7]

Chlorine doesn't stay very long in nature. As a gas it is poisonous for the respiratory system. Because of its high reactivity it combines with almost all elements; with some it forms salts. It is a halogen, meaning a builder of salt. Fluorine, bromine and iodine are all halogens. In us chlorine exists only as a chloride ion.

The chloride ion is very mobile and agitated in its behaviour. It has extreme reactivity and is everywhere in the ocean as well as in our internal fluids. According to the current scientific model, the main function of the chloride ion is to capture one more electron and form a loose ionic bond with many other substances. There's an ego-like activity here.

Another abundant substance in the ocean is sodium (Virgo manifestation, opposite Pisces in the zodiac), which is also highly reactive on the alkaline side. Sodium ion's main propensity is to donate an electron to a substance that needs one. Together the sodium and chloride ions form one of the main ocean salts (sodium chloride = table salt). When dissolved in water the ionic bond between these two is very loose and dissociation can occur fast in order for the chloride ion to attach itself to other substances. Because the link between sodium and chloride is weak when salt is diluted in water, the chloride ion can also decrease the salt content by linking with other substances. Then we have, in this chloride behaviour, one sphere of activity tending towards increased salt (crystallization), and another towards decreased salt (dissolution). The chloride ion enacts two alchemical processes. It is with that fragile balance that all creatures live. In Imma's drawing of Pisces we can see these two opposite tendencies so essential for all life forms.

The living being has to live with the right proportion of salt in its internal liquid. An important hormone in this regulation is aldosterone, produced by the glands sitting on the kidneys (adrenals). This hormone rules the blood salt level by telling the kidneys to reabsorb in the blood a limited quantity of sodium ions from the urine, and then the chloride ions follow.

Our stomach produces powerful hydrochloric acid when we eat. It acts as a second set of teeth to break food down. This acid puts a temporary stop to microbial growth and enhances enzymatic activities.

The chloride ion is essential to maintain the acid/base balance, to transmit nerve impulses and regulates fluid in and out of cells (osmotic pressure). Chloride ions (acid forming tendency) and sodium ions (alkaline forming tendency) are more abundant in the extra-cellular environment, whereas potassium and phosphate ions are more active inside cells. Cells expend a lot of energy to keep this balance right.

Mollusc: The Listening Foot

Molluscs — octopus, snails, oysters, bivalves:
45,000 species

Molluscs are among the first pluricellular animals to crawl on the earth and not just glide like the starfish. They move slowly on solid ground mainly in the oceans but also in our gardens.

'The name mollusc means "tough soft body". In most cases their body interior is soft but their external shells are very hard (lime). It is in that region between the soft body and the hard calcareous shell that the life of the mollusc is lived.'[8] The rem-

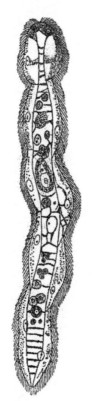

nants of their shells are numerous and have, over the aeons, formed mountain ranges through sedimentation (limestone). One of the key shapes or forms from these shells is the spiral.

In each animal, as in each of our organs, we can identify sensitive or neural activities, personalized rhythms and specific metabolic processes. For most vertebrates these activities have corporeal centres — head, thorax and abdomen. Molluscs, however, tend to perfect only one aspect of these three structures with different forms of feet.

The main ones are the 'head foot' (cephalopoda — octopus, cuttlefish). The eyes and the nervous system are highly developed. Some of them go backwards and forwards and change colours like a chameleon according to what they feel and for camouflage.

Some cephalopoda host strange ciliated vermiform parasites (Dicyemida which are five to ten millimetres in length) in their kidneys. They seem to live in octopus urine without harming their host. They have no body cavity, no differentiated organs, and have a reproductive cycle with male-female gametes. In their life cycle they have two embryonic stages (Fig. 1). They are strange

Fig. 1
Dicyemida
living in the
kidney of
octopus

animals with one long cell surrounded by much smaller ciliated cells. They do have a cephalic pole without a brain. They are quite enigmatic. Usually classed as parasites, do they in fact live in symbiosis with the octopus?

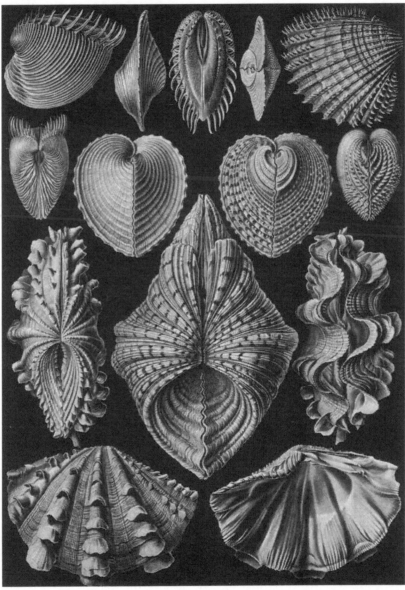

Fig. 2 Drawings of bivalves by E. Haeckel

There is another group without a brain (Acephala — mussels, bivalves) (Fig. 2). This group has a foot that paddles along the floor of the ocean. The two valves are an effective breathing system. Carbon dioxide (CO_2) reacts with calcium at the periphery, forming a huge variety of elegant colourful lime shells.

Fig. 3 Drawings of aquatic Gasteropoda by E. Haeckel

The third group are a 'stomach-foot' (Gasteropoda — slugs and snails) (Fig. 3). Here the metabolic process (digestion and reproduction) predominates.

With molluscs we see the start of a more complex system of organs which is the basis for more elaborate soul activities. These animals balance two organic tendencies in quite an original way:

1. They are highly proteinic, forming a large range of soft organ systems.
2. They deposit lime.

Harmony is established here between the living proteins and the mineral lime deposit.

With the Gasteropoda (snails) and their telescopic eyes we witness a huge variety of external forms with all sorts of coils and whirls in spirally triangular shapes. They are solidified vortices with an ability to produce a colourful porcelain finish.

To understand something of these shell forms we need to ask, what is a vortex? Our observation shows us that it is the primeval form where the states of matter are on the move. From oceanic currents to the vast weather systems of the earth, from galaxy nebulae to protein structures — it is all vortices. The Gasteropoda uses this primeval vortex expression to generate its own architecture.

We can put a mathematical formula on these spiralled parabolic curves and to do so we need the mathematical concept of infinity. Some representation of a particle is visualized as a kind of heart vortex shape made of very active lines of forces (Fig. 4).[9] Some organic forms have parabolic curves. They usually envelop the most contracted embryonic aspect of a living being. For plants it will be buds; for birds, eggs. These forms have parabolic curves linking infinity to the now. They are tridimensional listening curves.

Is it possible that these forms holding a germinal cell could be an aerial maintaining contact with the subtle influences of the spiritual world (Implicate order) in order for the embryo to develop properly?

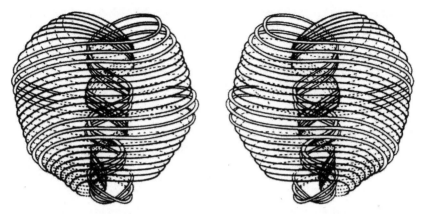

Fig. 4 Positive and negative ultimate particles in Occult Chemistry
(See Note 9)

To produce homeopathic remedies we dilute a substance and then shake the liquid (succussion). By doing so we generate millions of vortices. The French biologist Jacques Benveniste (1935–2004) demonstrated the fact that without succussion water doesn't register anything[10]. Only the creation of vortices can pick up the oscillating activity of a substance and transfer it into the water micro-structure.

With biodynamic preparations 500 and 501 that gather subtle influences over several months, a strong vortex shake up is needed to transfer the subtle influences to water. A vortex with its pulsing movement is seen as a listening form (ear) that can transfer (transducer) any kind of vibrations or oscillations into the subtle micro-structure of water.

Sense of Hearing

'Part of the human ear is formed like a snail shell. We can describe the snail and its shell as an ear, living life as a free-moving individual entity with certain necessary appendages. Among Protozoa Foraminifera there are many which resemble the mollusc form.'[11]

No ears without sounds, no eyes without light, and a newborn baby will have to be in touch with sound and light in the first two years of his life in order to develop the neurological connections with the brain. This includes movement of course. We are born as embryos and the first four years are crucial for the nervous, endocrine and immune system to start a coherent dialogue that will last the rest of our life.

Our ears are not just for sound reception. An organ of balance, filled with hair cells (statocysts), already present in echinoderm and Cnidarian, helps the primitive mollusc consciousness to relate with gravity (macula) and angular acceleration (crista ampullaris). It acts as an organ of equilibrium helping the organism to perceive its own balance against gravity. Later on in the vertebrates this balance and sound perception will be located in the ears.

Touching the Dense Ground: Foot

The octopus with its head with nearly perfected eyes, bivalves' rhythmic pulse roaming the ground of the ocean, and snail/ stomach crawling on the ground, have created various feet (poda) to touch the earth.

The term 'foot' means 'the beginning of the moment' in Marathi (Indo-Aryan language—India).[12] The feet ground us to Mother Earth while still in touch with cosmic influences. The junction of these two exists only in the present moment.

Jupiter Sphere Rules Pisces

An intention is at work in every building process inside or outside us. Every form is an expression of an intention. Seen this way forms become meaningful.

The mollusc goes a step further in developing sensory and motor apparatus and the external impressions need to be preserved by a more elaborate nerve and brain system. This is one aspect of the Jupiter metabolic process.

The other is the contribution of the liver (Jupiter's organ) in the constant recreation of personalized proteins for a spirit in incarnation, the establishment of an inner territory and its defence (immunity). Molluscs are highly proteinic creatures and the liver is well developed.

CONSONANT N

We have to develop the power of antipathy through engaging our forces with the earth, treading on it in order to move from one place to another.

'The healthy working in the soul of the N consonant can awaken the power in us to distinguish what is working over from the past, asking to be transformed into forces for the future. To awaken and grasp the moment of destiny is the message of the N.'[13]

Here we have two spheres, one from the past and one from the future, meeting in us in the eternity of the present moment. The sphere of the soul consciousness (psyche) is joined with the sphere of matter (physical form). The psyche has a constant need to discriminate.

Like the consonants D and T (Leo), the consonant N is a dental sound when the tongue meets the gum ridge and springs back. When saying 'no', the tongue touches the roof of the mouth and then quickly withdraws. There is a power of discrimination working here which is essential for the manifestation of one's destiny. It is our feet that lead us unconsciously towards our karma, and they embody the impulse of the sound N.

One of the primary activities of ancient man on earth was exchanging goods with other groups and sometimes they had to go into unknown territory and travel long distances. Steiner suggested that, as a primeval profession, the trader is linked with Pisces.[14]

Conclusion

Pisces gives us the instrument to walk on earth, touch the ground and move on it. The feet are a contact instrument summarizing the whole body. The formative forces of Pisces invite us to open and listen to the vibrations of the dense world. Molluscs develop multiple vortical aerials that can listen to subtle influences, prefiguring the ears.

The impulse of Pisces in living kingdoms shows the physical threefoldness (head, thorax and abdomen) of the future phyla, unfolding separately with feet.

Through its manifestation in the world of elements, the chloride ion can go in two opposite directions as in the drawing. Pisces establishes the right balance of salts essential for life on earth. In us chloride (Pisces) and sodium (Virgo) ions collaborate to maintain a balance between solubility and crystallization.

In the drawing, at a psychic level, one foot may represent our ego venture into matter, and the other one, walking and working on earth, invites us to go through discipleship towards the spiritual world. Discipleship here refers to the capacity the spirit in us has to master the forces of our lower soul astrality that we share with the animals in order to create a direct rapport with the spiritual world via the higher self.

The mollusc group develops the liver and the nervous system to a high degree compared to the previous phyla.

6. Aquarius

Preamble

Imma's drawings were strongly influenced by the fact that she meditated for a year at sunrise on the constellation behind the sun. In the course of 1911, Steiner followed her closely giving specific instructions. Very little is known about these conversations.

Imma's drawings are pictures of the formative aspect of the stars. They are super-sensible influences coming to earth. We are not only receiving a sub-sensible world of frequencies we are familiar with (radio, TV or microwaves), we are also constantly being influenced by these supra-earthly aspects.

Whatever time of the day there is always a constellation raining down super-sensible influences on us behind the sun. Has the sun a role to play in the transmission of these formative influences?

Steiner invited scientists to keep an open mind about this very hot entity. Many instruments are turned towards its extreme activity. Their findings start more questions than answers as to the nature of the sun.

Steiner mentioned that scientists 'would be very astonished if they were to get near [the sun]; they would not find fine fiery gas but they would find something ... that is a vacuum that exerts suction ... The fine etheric structure of the universe, which is also spiritual, is continuously sucked in by the sun as nourishment.'[1]

He said the sun is 'a hollowed-out form in space', a kind of 'big hole' in the fabric of the space-time continuum where space relates with counter space, or other dimensions. The constellations' formative influences 'are drawn in by the super-suction of the sun, by that hole in space'.[2] This hole is 'a suction sphere ... really a vacuum or empty space, nay even less than empty, negative matter'.[3] In this context the sun appears as an entry and exit point connecting the Implicate order of spiritual activities with the Explicate order of the kingdoms of nature.

What came out of Imma's meditations are drawings with an intuitive understanding. The ancients' way to represent the constellation through glyph and picture is correct. Man's interest in the past was oriented towards the impact of the stars on his own psyche, or the way he organized his life. Imma's drawings are new ways to see the nature of these forces and orient us towards the archetypal vector of activities constantly forming nature's manifestation. Will humanity in the future be able to use these formative forces to build new technologies that are not harmful for nature and human beings? A technology friendly to life?

The Constellation of Aquarius (The Waterman)

Content

This text explores the imprint of the intelligent activity of Aquarius all around us in the constant forming of human and animal creation. What is the relation between the Aquarius sector of space, its glyph, the medieval image of this constellation,

Imma's drawing, the element oxygen, the animal phylum Vermes, the warmth sense, the legs, Uranus as a ruling planet, the colour red and the consonant M? Based on Imma's drawings in the first edition of *The Calendar of the Soul* in 1912, we can find a golden thread linking the various ways Aquarius acts as a constant blueprint in nature.

Description of the Glyph

The glyph itself reminds us of flowing waves, two lines undulating with synchronicity. A space is contained between these two lines but open on both sides as if the external world passes through and is transformed. You could also imagine it like a representation of a wavy cylinder.

The traditional pictures showed someone pouring water on earth from one, sometimes two, jars, suggesting free-flowing fertility.

Description of the Drawing

This drawing has ardour, a fiery movement. A flowing energy where one aspect of the drawing seems to generate another. The top left has a lighter maze structure than the dark turbulent bottom right.

The four dark watery whirls go upwards connecting with other forms. They connect with the centre form with its theatrical appearance—a kind of being flaming up joyfully in the air towards the centre of the drawing.

The general background on the right of this luminous creature is dark, punctuated with channels. It seems as if a crawling multitude is in action here. The left side of this drawing, in continuity with the dark whirls, is more organized. It looks like ancient runes or a labyrinthine fabric alongside segmented tubular structures.

Oxygen: Let the Energy Flow

Another way to see these dark whirls is to imagine them as representative of the plant kingdom, like sprouts of primitive plants such as fern crosses. It is out of the photosynthesis process that oxygen for the first time is freed in the air and water. Oxygen represents this luminous form at the centre of the drawing. In nature photosynthesis is the dynamic process that captures sunlight to build a carbohydrate architecture (plant). The plant uses a bit of this oxygen because it breathes, though it is mainly animals that use it. Respiration is the counterpart of photosynthesis where the carbohydrates are dismantled providing the energy to produce the proteinic forms of animals.

'Oxygen made the earth a living planet that attracts in her the life of the cosmos. It is the element for the incarnation of the etheric body.'[4]

In Goethean terms, oxygen 'is the bearer of forces whereby "Being" becomes "appearance"'. It is a life-generating substance (biogen) that brings movement. In this drawing we have this glorious movement. 'Oxygen enlivens every earthly organism.'[5]

Emerging from these whirls is this flaming oxygen shape bringing the possibility for animal expression. Our blood has a great longing for oxygen. Specific centres in our reptilian brain produce our automatic breathing. The first breath of a newborn is a longing for life. Without oxygen there is no freeing of energy in our mitochondria (the little furnaces inside the cells) and no protein construction or movement.

The traditional image for Aquarius is a man pouring water with profusion on to the ground. Water has always been the best mover of matter and carries subtle influences. In the zodiac the polar opposite of Aquarius is Leo which manifests as hydrogen in the world of the elements. When joined together they create water in the same way as Pisces (chlorine) and Virgo (sodium) create the main salt of the ocean. We are made of 70 per cent salty water without which we couldn't live. Ocean water is our primeval serum and similar to our own blood serum. Remember, the echinoderm still use sea-water as their blood serum.

Vermes: the Undulated Tubular Ones

Vermes: 30,000 species

Vermes is the old name given to long cylindrical invertebrates (flat or round) with muscular pulses bringing food from mouth to anus. They can be segmented like the earthworm or not. Today biologists have separated them into numerous phyla. They don't glide or walk on the surface but dig tunnels into the earth or any fleshy substance in need of digestion.

If we imagine the four dark whirls on Imma's drawing as being represented in perspective we can see that they are the same size. In which case they can be seen as segments of the same long movement. Annelida (earthworms) show a well-developed metamerized (segmented) body. Which means that segmentation is external as well as internal. We also see, on the left side of the drawing, a stylistic representation of these creatures attributed to Aquarius. The tendency towards segmented organs is an important step in the evolution of more complex animals. Very early in the human embryo we observe this primitive segmentation called somites or metameres developing into bilateral segments. These segments give rise to most of the muscular-skeletal system.

They can live as parasites in other creatures or dig the soil by eating what is in front of them. Doing so, Vermes leave behind them a multitude of fertile tunnels in the soil. In the left side of the drawing we observe the labyrinthine matrix they build. The Annelid like the earthworm is a good example of this group.

The food we eat is not truly 'inside' us but in muscular tubes between the mouth and the anus. This whole gastrointestinal tract is a workshop of organs with strong wavy peristaltic movements. Through enzymatic activities they work hard to separate the pure (the soluble) from the impure (the insoluble).

For instance, we can't digest cellulose (fibres). This work is done in the large intestine with a huge variety of tiny creatures. Some of them are the multiple forms of the same bacteria that work as the digestive system of the biosphere.

Associated with plant roots, bacteria organize the earth minerals (metals) into soluble compounds that the plants integrate into their cellulose architecture. These are the ashes when we burn wood. In the large intestine, through fermentation, the bacteria free the minerals for us to absorb. We must never underestimate the power of these micro-minerals (oligo elements) that micro-organisms free in our gut. Without these micro elements the building tools (enzymes) are very sluggish. We are literally doped with about a dozen various metals such as cobalt, manganese, copper etc. to increase the efficiency of our organs' inner processes.

The Sense of Warmth

Our own sense of warmth is very suggestive. Something is cold or warm according to our internal temperature in an area of the body. Let us suppose the right hand is in icy water and the left hand in hot water. Then both hands are plunged into water at room temperature. The right hand feels warm and the left hand cold.

By its oxidizing power (no fire without oxygen), and by its collaboration in the creation of water, Aquarius is a sign of flowing energy. The formative forces of Aquarius invite organic matter of all kinds to flow and transform. This drawing has a definite quality of abundant mixing and brewing.

The Greek element fire is heat state coupled with the warmth ether. Heat is a maestro of ceremonies that allows the movement of matter from gas to liquid to solid according to the amount of heat in them. Heat expands things and penetrates everything bringing a tendency towards levity. In the animal kingdom oxygen frees the imprisoned heat and light and makes it available for the creation of proteins and movement. In us, as in nature, all sorts of dynamic systems are present to maintain the right degree of warmth essential for life.

There is a warm, even fiery, sympathetic presence in the drawing.

Legs

'With the legs there is a meeting of the warmth of the body with the external warmth.'[6]

We know that at the calves the bloodstream comes to an area where we can lose heat. For instance, in the case of fever, a wet cloth on the calf can help bring the temperature down.

The legs have several muscles and the large calf muscle is made of two bellies joining in the Achilles tendon at the foot. Leg muscles activate the use of the feet and toes. Steiner said that this part of our body is embryonic and will go through many changes before becoming an organ of active creation in the future.

'Our legs from the knees downwards are immersed in the etheric body of the earth.'[7]

Via the legs and feet there is a constant flow of subtle energy through us. Walking all the time on bitumen or concrete surfaces undermines this flow.

Uranus Rules Aquarius

Uranus is beyond Saturn. It doesn't impact directly on our metabolic process like the other planets between the sun and Saturn. Uranus, Neptune and Pluto seem to have been caught up later after the formation of the solar system and influence the metabolic processes through the human psyche. Uranus was first seen around the time of the French Revolution, with its erratic course around the sun over a period of 84 years, which is the predicted life span of man in the next Aquarian Age.[8]

People influenced by this energy can have sudden, erratic changes of mind, spontaneous reversals that produce emotional waves in them and others. This drawing shows waves producing other forms. So many sudden reversals of weather patterns (Ice Ages) have accompanied evolution on earth each time bringing new expressions of life in their aftermath. After every Ice Age life returned with new complex forms.

CONSONANT: M

The Aquarius glyph looks like the consonant M.

'With M we can produce a continuous flow of air until the lungs are empty of breath making the lips and the belly vibrate. The consonant M is a kind of doorway between vowels and consonants. It is a sound of sympathy and devotion.'[9]

That is what the Vermes initiate: a continuous flow through peristaltic vibrations.

Conclusion

With oxygen the energy flows. Within pulsing tubular space matter flows too.

It is the impulse of Aquarius to generate for the first time in the animal realm these long cylindrical worms, flat or round, parasitic or not, segmented or not, elastic muscular beings with a beginning (mouth) and an end (anus). They are digestive systems bringing the flow of digested liquid in one direction, a bit like our own segmented intestine with its peristaltic movement.

Another important tubular/elastic/muscular structure in us that allows the movement of liquid is our blood vessels with a muscular tone impacting on the blood pressure. Blood is the only tissue flowing rhythmically into the intimacy of each organ allowing matter and subtle influences to flow.

When we touch a worm it tends to coil like the coils in Imma's drawing. The dark right-hand side of the drawing can be compared to a fertile plot of land full of tunnels created by the activities of earthworms. Darwin wrote a whole book praising earthworms for generating fertile ground. The glyph can be seen as moving worms or the peristaltic movement of the digestive tract.

It is interesting to look at the larva stage of these creatures. Evolution of form starts at the embryonic level because of the greater gene plasticity. In Vermes, as in the Molluscs, the trochophore larva and its transformation into veliger larva (mollusc), (that live in abundance in the ocean plankton), are at the start of the metamorphosis process where a form becomes another one.

Metamorphosis is something that greatly puzzles scientists. It makes sense only if we recognize an intelligent activity working through the emergence of forms.

7. Capricorn

Preamble

We are accustomed to qualify the vibrations of sound and the sub-world of the electromagnetic spectrum with frequencies. One vibration in a second is one hertz. The light in our home, because of the alternating current, flickers on and off 50 times per second or 50 hertz. This is a very low frequency compared with gamma and cosmic rays with their millions of vibrations per second. But what do we call a vibration or pattern of activity that occurs every two seconds, every minute or even every eight years like the dance of Venus around the earth? Is it a pulsation, a recurring momentum, an oscillation? And, like any choreography, it must be an activity with a meaning. It represents a kind of intelligent activity.

Astronomers talk a lot about star movements, their electromagnetic activities and the tremendous speed of galaxies. From earth we perceive the constellations as they come and go, turning around us as if we were inside a gigantic dynamic clock. Sometimes their influences are obscured by the moon and sometimes their formative forces are amplified by the sun. We live inside constantly pulsing rhythms. Because of the earth's motion within the solar system, we have days, seasons and geological periods. Nothing is static but everything has an organized momentum. Our time scale is based on this movement. Our galaxy and solar system move at 500,000 km/hour towards the Hercules constellation. If we know now that matter is never at rest why is it that most religions still imagine a spirit world as a frigidly unmoving realm eternally static?

In the rhythm of the natural world around us we perceive movements of contraction and expansion (night – day, winter – summer). The etheric nature of our being manifests in this way in order to create us. This is due to the constant increase and decrease of warmth and light.

Rhythms are not energy or matter but are essential for a spirit to manifest its threefold form in matter, (see Virgo chapter) to create a vehicle that becomes, for a time, a creature in the king-doms of nature. Life is rhythm said Steiner. What we perceive is the expression of life, not life itself. The twelve constellations are pulsing entities that contain intelligent intentions to direct nature towards particular directions. For Capricorn, that direction is to articulate various parts of the body.

The Constellation of Capricorn (Goat/Fish)

Content

This text explores the imprint of the intelligent activity of Capricorn all around us in the constant forming of human and animal creation. What is the relation between the Capricorn sector of space, its glyph, the medieval image of this constella-tion, Imma's drawing, the element aluminium, the animal phy-lum Arthropoda, the sense of sight, the knee, Saturn as a ruling planet, the colour peach-blossom and the consonant L? Based on Imma's drawings in the first edition of *The Calendar of the Soul* in

1912, we can try to find a golden thread linking the various ways Capricorn acts as a constant blueprint in nature.

Description of the Glyph

No other sign of the zodiac has its glyph represented in so many different ways. In all the variations there is a common denominator: they express mobility or a tendency to establish a link between one part that is above and another below. It is often a cup shape with a line going down and another up, finishing with a loop. It suggests a connection between two things.

The traditional picture has an earthy aspect with a goaty front body (hard and dry), as well as a watery whirly fish tail at the end. There is versatility in this symbolic picture. It is also seen as half animal with a human torso like the centaur. The goat-fish, as well as the centaur, is a symbol of our physical and psychic animality.

Description of the Drawing

Many whirly movements are present in this dark agitated drawing. Everything seems to whirl around a central sketchy creature. Its presence among the brouhaha shows three distinct parts: a head-like organization with prominent eyes, a suggested nose and a bushy mouth. Two swirls emerge from inbetween the eyes and sit above the head like aerials.

Below the head with its sensorial apparatus there is a horizontal movement. If we start from the centre of the left whirl we see a clockwise movement that links with the right whirl. If we start from the centre of the right we see an anticlockwise movement. This suggests a rhythmic oscillation.

From the left central oscillating whirl we see a long wavy movement branching off at the end into a fish tail and surrounded by a bustle of activities on the right.

Finally, the bottom part stands like a dark watery pool with three strong vortical actions. Did this creature come out of the water? The whole dark background is peppered with vortical formative activities as if an invisible hand acts in the air behind the scene.

Aluminium: The Plasticity of Forms

The numerous whirlwinds that seem so hurly-burly in this dark background, like the potter's work, remind us of the plasticity and water absorption of aluminium when associated with silica (to form clay). There is no fertile ground without it.

'Clay is responsive to formative forces (fingers) working on it from outside. Just as a musical instrument responds to a musician, so plastic clay is the instrument for the music of forms composed by the sculptor.'[1]

Aluminium, the most abundant metal in the earth's crust, is not free-standing in nature but rather combines in manifold ways. Its main association is with silica in rocks (such as feldspar). It is also present in most precious stones. In fertile soil it brings plasticity (clay) and water absorption as well as retention.

In human ashes we find silica and aluminium, but physiologists don't fully understand why. Are they just pollutants that we store? It is only relatively recently (c. 1880s), with the use of electricity, that we have been able to extract pure aluminium metal from bauxite. Our internal environment is more in touch with it through cooking in aluminium pots. The acidification of the soil can also release aluminium into fertile ground.

If silica (Aries) goes through us and lodges itself at the periphery of membranes and organisms as a transmitter of subtle influences, and if phosphorus (Cancer) gives surface sensibility to plants and animals, then aluminium introduces plasticity. We have aluminium in us in a very small quantity acting as an activity more than a substance.

Arthropoda: The Articulated One

Arthropoda — insect, spider, scorpion, lobster ... :
1,000,000 species

Imma's drawing of Capricorn shows a three-part being as a directional impulse. Centres for neural function, pulsating rhythm and transformation of substance start to articulate and unify in one organism. 90 per cent of animal species on earth are in these varied phyla — insect, spider, scorpion, lobster, crab. The head, thorax and abdomen are serial articulated units (metamere structure).

The Arthropoda shows a segmented, mobile, chitinous exo-skeleton with legs and wings ever adaptable and pliable. Like the glyph, all articulations have an element of concavity and con-vexity. The Arthropodes were the first to explore these new articulated possibilities.

'It is difficult to say which of the two, the over-plastic or the over-rigid, appears the more weird to man.'[2]

Sense of Sight

The sensibility of plant cells to light is well known (heliotrop-ism). Creatures that want to move more freely in space need to link light perception with movement because light reveals space. In the development of phyla the spirit in incarnation desires an apparatus. Very early on a primitive eye develops, even at an embryonic level. It reaches near perfection with the octopus. Arthropoda explored the eyes to an extravagant degree from simple light receptors to complex compound eyes perceiving diverse aspects of the light phenomena from infra-red to ultra-violet rays.

What more is there to say about these huge eyes and aerials in Imma's drawing? The various species of Arthropoda will develop their capacity to perceive light in numerous ways. In this phylum, as in the drawing, the tactile antennae start around the eyes, opening these animals to specific aspects of the electro-magnetic spectrum signals (infrared or ultraviolet). Each species has its specific antenna and there are hundreds of thousands of aerial types.

Entomologist Philip S. Callahan has put forth the controversial idea that insects have a generalized high sensitivity to the infrared energy spectrum perfectly designed to optimize the transmission and detection of free-floating scent molecules by 'pumping' them into a coherent non-linear infrared emission phase through the use of sound. He states, 'as long as sound is studied in one corner of the lab and scent in another, the mechanisms of these sound-modulated scent molecules will not be understood'. Bees are one insect species well known to per-ceive and use ultraviolet.

What kind of consciousness accompanies compound eyes?

'It must be a self-abandonment of the individual in a directionless multiplicity of all possible focal points or, as a mathematician might put it, a facing of the "infinity far plane" which surrounds our world.'[2]

Fig. 1 Photo of insect compound eyes

Their compound eyes see a decomposed space, or bits of information about space like serial linear units of pixels (Fig. 1).

Self-abandonment is also there for us if we want to observe anything. If someone walks on a forest path but is busy in his mind sorting out a problem (e.g. anxiety), he won't see anything. The eyes are open, the visual information enters subliminally but doesn't reach the con-sciousness. Self-abandonment to sense the world is a heart decision to shut down the mental and observe. Then our inner light will meet the outer light. In this way the eyes are formed in the embryo: an internal membrane movement comes to meet an external movement coming in.

In Imma's drawing, we can see a sort of tail branching off over the pool. It can be said that the main function of a fish tail is propulsion. It seems that out of this whirling activity in the pool the creature in the drawing is propelled into gravity, into the air element. The nose of this threefold being is suggesting a passage from water to air. Of course, creatures of the air, like insects or spiders, are not breathing through a nose; their lung is in the abdomen. Only in the air can we smell: in water, animals taste. The phylum insect represents the majority of all the animal species and they rely on smell for the running of their instinctual behaviour.

Because of their lightness the pull of gravity is not so great for them. The insects invaded the air about the same time as the plant kingdom propagated on solid ground, establishing strong symbiotic links that last to this day. The insects also started to generate various sounds with their articulated body parts (such as crickets and cicadas still do today).

Knee

In medieval pictures of man Capricorn influences the knee which is the mobile connection between our lower leg (Aquarius) and thigh (Sagittarius). As one of our biggest joints, and vital for our mobility in the outside world, the knee is a symbol of the whole articulated system animating our skeleton. Even the bones of the cranium have a kind of motion between them. This is what articulation is about. The constellation of Capricorn points to the knee as a symbol of the various ways the bones connect with one another to give us greater flexibility.

In the complex Capricorn glyph we sense a will to establish a link between two aspects. The cup shape at the top is a container that receives subtle energy. This energy enters and mingles with our own.

'The knee is the area where the ether currents of the outer world (the earth) enter into individual currents of the human being's own ether body'[3] after going through the feet and legs that act as captors of earth energy.

Saturn sphere rules Capricorn

The Saturn sphere invites the life of senses[4] at the periphery of the body. Specialized organs of perception develop with the Arthropoda to have a better apprehension of the outside world. The sense of sight already exists in more primitive creatures but with the articulated Arthropoda we reach a summit of variations.

It is the Saturn impact on animality that stimulates the opening of doors of perception (sense organs) to the multitudinous aspects of the outer world. Capricorn creates articulations between different parts to increase mobility. The sense of sight, omnipresent in Arthropoda, enormously favours flexible movements in space.

This Saturn sphere of activity tends to harmonize the outside and inside rhythms. It helps the integration of outside rhythmic stimuli inside an autonomous rhythmic organism. The subtle aspect of the spleen (the Saturn organ) does that in us.[5]

The Consonant L

The consonant L 'is a sound swinging in the element of life' or 'a force relationship between man's limbs and the earth'.[6] A sound between a vowel and a consonant 'lifting us out of gravity'.[7]

Imma's drawing shows a creature that is about to experience life outside water by being propelled into the air. In water things have the same mass but weigh much less. For instance, our brain weighs 50g floating in our brain fluid, whereas on a scale it weighs 1500g. Arthropoda outside water are small (insects, spiders, etc.) and don't experience the full pull of gravity.

Conclusion

The Capricorn impulse articulates three structural centres with limbs into a unity that serves the emergence of soul faculties. Saturn gives them, through multiple ways to use eyes, the chance to experience movement in space more fully. Percepts and articulated movements come together more strongly with these varied groups of animals.

Some look clumsy and robotic with their instinctual drives (lobsters), whereas others have a more elegant fragile pliability — butterflies. Sometimes they dance in the air as a soul-group bringing a choreographic expression of their animal soul-group (a bee swarm).

The articulated external skeleton, made of chitin shields and rods with a ventral neural system, will reverse with the vertebrates into an internal articulated bone structure with dorsal neural system.

Through their many ways to sense the external world Arthropoda harmonize their internal rhythms with the external ones — an aspect of the Saturn metabolic process.

8. Sagittarius

Preamble

In the intimacy of our daily life we don't easily notice the vast pulsations of the dynamic cosmic clock we live by: that the sun goes anticlockwise through the zodiac over a period of 25,920 years needs centuries of observation. That the planets seen from earth trace a loopy pathway taking many years to complete would need long periods of careful observations. Nevertheless, ancient cultures were able to detect these pulsing rhythmic activities.

The main pulsing rhythms obvious to us are expressed in days and seasons. These pulses, due to earth's movements around itself and the sun, accompany the threefold construction of plants (root, stem/leaves and flower/seed) and animals (head, thorax and abdomen). We notice that in order for this three-foldness to appear in space there is a need for a time process. This is simple observation.

The five Chinese HUA or movements (wood, fire, earth, metal and water) express among other things this cyclical time process. These HUA have nothing at all to do with the four Greek elements and were incorrectly translated as five 'elements' by the first translators of Chinese texts on physiology. These texts used ideograms that express more the idea of an activity and never a concept which makes their translations difficult. It is like converting a poetic text on human physiology into a modern scientific language. The ideograms of the five HUA represent *a cyclical movement of metamorphosis through the constant increase and decrease of the light and warmth of the sun on a daily and seasonal basis.* This time cycle has a profound impact on all the kingdoms of nature.

The plant emerges from a *point*—seed or bud. This is germination (*wood movement*) where *lines* of expression open in a vertical spiral gesture as roots and stems. Then the plant establishes itself in space with the rhythmic unfolding of *surfaces* with its leaves (*fire movement*). Maturity brings the growth of *volume* with flowers (*earth movement*). This last stage (fertilization) assures a future. In maturing, the seeds go into a desiccating process (*metal movement*) where the future germ is surrounded by compounds (oil and protein) essential for the next germination. Then the dry seeds disseminate and begin a period of dormancy in the ground (*water movement which is a return to the origin*). These five movements sum up the cycle of the plant. The basis of all geometry is here.

In animals, life starts with a germ (*contraction – water*) that expands into embryo/young (*opening into existence – wood*). Next we observe a full growth (*expansion in space – fire*). Like the flower stage, the animal reaches maturity and can reproduce (*contribution to the future of the species – earth*). The last stage we observe is old age (*a drying out process – metal*). With the animal expression again we have the five HUA[1]. We don't see life. We perceive its rhythms. What we see of life is its manifold manifestations. Life is never a mechanical rhythm but a dynamic one full of various pulses.

Earth's ecosystem rhythmically expands in spring-summer and contracts in autumn-winter. This is also the way the etheric world works outside and inside us. Plants and animals have various responses to this cycle (plants bloom and wither, animals hibernate and migrate, etc).

Being smaller than nature, these five cycles reverberate much faster within human beings. To look at this cyclical movement within us we need to observe the only tissue that flows into the intimacy of each organ: the blood. Each organ influences the blood stream in a certain way many times a day.

For example: when the blood leaves the kidneys it loses heat, gases, liquids and various organic and mineral substances – this is urine. The kidneys, with their seed shape, constantly contract (water movement) the blood stream. No other organ reduces the blood like that to its essential mineral/organic content. Other organs are more involved in expanding the blood stream. This is the subject of another book.

The Constellation of Sagittarius (Archer)

Content

This text explores the imprint of the intelligent activity of Sagittarius around us in the constant forming of human and animal creation. What is the relation between the Sagittarius sector of space, its glyph, the medieval image of this constellation, Imma's drawing, the element magnesium, the animal phylum fishes, the taste sense, the thigh, Jupiter as a ruling planet, the colour rose-lilac and the consonants K and G? Based on Imma's drawings in the first edition of *The Calendar of the Soul* in 1912, we can find a golden thread linking the various ways Sagittarius acts as a constant blueprint in nature.

Description of the Glyph and Traditional Picture

In the glyph we have an arrow pointing obliquely in a diagonal direction. The traditional picture shows a centaur with an arrow in tension on a bow pointing in one direction. The centaur is an image of the human being emerging slowly from its animal nature.

Description of the Drawing

The drawing shows a distinct vertical figure shooting out of the water where two whirls are seen on the surface.

On the shore of this patch of water behind the figure we see a rocky animal form resting like the Egyptian Sphinx.

From the water, like leaping arrows, two nearly vertical curves unite and give rise to two horizontal wings organizing the middle part of the drawing. The whole thing has a feeling of propulsion ending with flapping wings agitating the air below. These two vertical/horizontal central movements form an incomplete hollow at the centre where the human head of the Sphinx should be seen.

The human head of the Sphinx is not present in this drawing but instead a more animal-like mask is above suggesting a new direction of development towards more complex vertebrates. The word Sphinx comes from the Egyptian word *Shesepankh* meaning a living image. The Sphinx was created a long time before the pyramids, carved on the spot out of a single rock. Imma's drawing shows this rocky sculpture on a shore. It is known today that the basis of the Egyptian Sphinx was eroded by water. The centaur and the Sphinx are each half human half animal.

Then from this hollow between the wings a head form emerges and irradiates the top of the drawing with strong slanted eyes and a suggestion of a nose and mouth. In this hollow the glyph of Aries emerges suggesting a face.

Magnesium: a Lightning Element

Magnesium is the substance used in the old-fashioned camera flashes. When it burns it has a dazzling irradiating light that can overcome the sunlight. The head mask in the drawing has this sort of irradiation. Magnesium itself has the role of a light propellant and is abundant in seeds to propel their new manifestation. It also sits at the centre of the chlorophyll pigment essential to capture light in the vegetal kingdom. Magnesium propels light into the the plant kingdom. In nature it often appears as magnesium silicate, as in the minerals serpentine and asbestos that tend to form a fibrous structure. In this drawing the head shows clearly this fibrous tendency to ray out. As magnesium oxide it is a solid that can hold a high temperature (2000 degrees centigrade). In association with sulphur magnesium sulphate forms 16 per cent of ocean salts.[2]

In humans, in a very small quantity, it acts as a co-factor of enzymatic activities. Located inside cells it regulates the salt content (sodium pump) and acts on molecules that carry energy (ATP–ADP). The fulcrum point of magnesium in the blood is ruled by aldosterone from the adrenals acting on the kidneys.

Fishes: The Arrow-Like Creatures

Fishes: 25,500 species

The phylum fish is the first chordata group which has a vertebral column with a head. With his male/female head in meditation facing the sunrise, the Sphinx is an image of the animal on its way to the human. It is also an image of a listening heart.

The bottom part of this drawing with its whirly water is what is actually happening in the primitive ocean. One thing that is represented here is the beginning of the chordata venture (animal with a vertebral column/cranium). Sagittarius continues what has been started in Aries with the tunicata. We can see the Aries sign in the opening of the hollow formed by the wings.

With Aries we have the development of the phylum tunicata classified as pro-chordata because they don't form an inner skeleton. These are among the first group of animals, during the Cambrian explosion[3] to generate a notochord. Some are still

living embryos in the ocean today (lancelet). Man shares with all
the chordata this embryonic stage with a notochord, which is a
kind of primitive cartilaginous backbone that synchronizes the
formation of the neural tube in the embryo. The neural tube is the
precursor of the central nervous system. The interior of our
cartilaginous intervertebral discs is called the nucleus pulposa
and is the remnant of the notochord.

With Sagittarius we see the emergence of the first real chordata: the multiple varieties of fishes. Some of them stay cartilaginous (sharks) but most of them develop bones. The two vertical
movements in the drawing, uniting with the two horizontal
flapping ones, may be seen as masses of muscles activating the
wings. What is the shape of a fish? We can see it as a head-thigh
moving like a directed arrow, as in the Sagittarius glyph.

Being practically weightless in water fishes don't need wings
but only fins that help them to fly/glide in the liquid element and
stabilize their position in connection with the light gravity they
perceive. The whole fish form is an organ of propulsion not very
different from our thighs. Both contain powerful muscles. These
skeletal muscles are made of long, multinucleate cellular fibres
giving them a structure like the two vertical fibrous movements
in the drawing.

Sense of Taste

Invertebrate animals have a diffuse nervous system, autonomous
in nature, with several nervous ganglia ruling diverse basic
functions. Added to that the chordata fishes initiate a central
nervous system protected inside a flexible bony structure (ver-
tebrae/cranium). Because of that, their sensorial and motor
systems give rise to more complex instinctual behaviours.
Creatures in the air can smell. Animals in the ocean can't; they
taste, and the invertebrates develop it to various degrees. With
fishes we see the development of a very keen sense of taste
spread through their skin and gills. Salmon living in the ocean

can find their way to the river where they were spawned just by tasting the river flowing into the ocean.

'The stripes down the side [lateral lines] exist to make them subtly sensitive to the light and warmth in their environment. . . . It is therefore a kind of nerve organ.'[4]

An Organ of Propulsion: Thigh

The thigh, with its powerful set of muscles, is designed to help us leap or spring forwards. It is very useful for taking us in a particular direction. These muscles activate the leg (Aquarius) with the knee articulation (Capricorn).

Jupiter Sphere Rules Sagittarius

With Jupiter the life of nerves is essential to preserve the impressions received. The brain, which is made of nerves, increases its density and organization enormously with these first vertebrates.

The liver metabolic process is strongly involved in the organization of the inner territory (connective tissue) and defence (immunity). The liver helps the incarnated spirit to produce its unique set of proteins by juggling with organic matter.

Consonants: K, G, NG, CH

In the centre of the drawing there is a kind of tight hollow, a bit like a sphincter, where the flapping of the wings open and close, The word sphincter derives from the Greek verb *sphingo* meaning to squeeze, to tighten up. To make the consonants K and G we need to contract our abdominal muscles to increase air pressure, and at the same time block the air coming out by contracting the soft palate and tongue, the sudden opening of which can generate the K or G. By doing so we create a kind of sphincter link with air pressure.

In the drawing, at the meeting of the two wings, there is a sort of squeezing where the head suddenly pops out. The face in the drawing expresses an earthly animality in place of the listening human head facing the sunrise of the original Sphinx.

Conclusion

The opposite of Sagittarius is Gemini. Gemini brings in the first pluricellular creatures, a dual structure by initiating lateral bisymmetry. With Sagittarius we tend towards a unity of direction within this symmetry. In water the fishes, as the first vertebrates, have the speed and versatility of an arrow while keeping the bilateral symmetry.

Fishes come with so many forms and colours. In general they are a concentration of strong muscles with a head—e.g. the salmon. They are designed to propel themselves forward. Their internal muscular-skeletal system is predominantly helping them to shoot ahead. The propulsion can be powerful, as with a shark, or when the soul-group inhabits the multitude they become one entity dancing in water like starlings in the air. This tendency to congregate together and act as one soul-group is present in all the phyla.

Experiencing slight gravity in water, fishes don't need wings but gentle fins to stay upright in water. Some of them like birds develop wing-like structures (e.g. sting ray).

Speaking of wings, the constellation of Sagittarius is flanked by two bird constellations: Aquila, the eagle—symbol of immortality or of the spirit manifesting through the soul, and Cygnus the swan with its four stars in the form of a cross, symbolizing the soul crucified in matter.

9. Scorpio

Preamble

The study of rock strata and their content was well on its way in the nineteenth century. What astonished geologists is the fact that the Cambrian stratum contains so many fossils of various multicelled animals. They called it the Cambrian explosion or radiation. All of a sudden, seemingly without any warning in the geological record, representatives of most invertebrates appeared, including the tunicata (pro-chordata). A huge mass diversification of complex phyla popped up over a comparatively short period of time. English naturalist Charles Darwin (1809–1882) was well aware of this and said it was one of the main objections to be made against the theory of evolution by natural selection. He remained very puzzled by the problem his entire life.

Before the Cambrian era there were only single-celled animals and plants. One thing seems sure, the emergence of plants (algae) created a milieu with more oxygen in the seawater. This is essential for more complex animal forms, and the Protozoa had time to purify and clarify the original muddy soup of the primeval oceans through sedimentation of calcium and silica.

It is not just this Cambrian explosion that poses problems for the theory of evolution through natural selection. We now know that there have been at least five mass extinction events in the geological past on earth. These mass extinctions were devastating to living species. It is estimated that 80 per cent of known species both alive and extinct (plants and animals) are now part of fossil records.

Exactly how did new phyla emerge so quickly following these catastrophic events? Biologists have to cope with the fact that major new chromosomic sequences appeared faster than they would have expected. If it is just a matter of random mutation, then they have a probability problem.

Consider one of the early evolutionary steps, the passage from fish to frog. There are thousands of genes to handle, thousands of generations which must have necessarily taken a very long time.

We can ask: how long will it take for a monkey to write a Shakespearian sonnet by typing at random on a keyboard with 26 letters? The answer is more aeons than the presumed age of our universe. Hence the probability problem with a purely random evolutionary theory.

The thesis presented here opens the possibility for understanding the constant dialogue between the activities of nature and the surrounding cosmos. In this vast dynamic cosmic clock we live in, there seem to be windows of opportunity for new happenings. Fresh influxes of subtle influences allowed new beginnings or transitions, be it chromosomic changes or earthly movements. Most of the genetic material of a cell (80 per cent) is what scientists call 'junk' DNA. By focusing only on chromosomes and their genes we are in danger of discarding a very important aspect of this apparently dormant genetic material and its capacity to be influenced by super-sensible directional forces.

As well as five major extinctions we can identify several minor ones in the geological record. Each time, life manifests again with more complex forms of animals and plants. Mammals were present during the Mesozoic era alongside dinosaurs. Small creatures, similar to meerkats and rats, living in the subsoil of the tropical forest, they couldn't match the size and ferocity of the dinosaurs. Then a major extinction event happened that changed the whole climate. The old reptilian expression of the dinosaurs could no longer survive. From that time onwards the warm-blooded animals (bird and mammal) could express themselves in all their extravagance.

'The one thing she [nature] seems to aim at is Individuality; yet she cares nothing for the individuals. She is always building up and destroying; but her workshop is inaccessible.'[1]

The Constellation of Scorpio (Eagle/Scorpion)

Content

This text explores the imprint of the intelligent activity of Scorpio around us in the constant forming of human and animal creation. What is the relation between the Scorpio sector of space, its glyph, the medieval image of this constellation, Imma's drawing, the element carbon, the animal phylum amphibian, the sense of smell, the genitalia, Mars as a ruling planet, the colour lilac and the consonant S? Based on Imma's drawings in the first edition of *The Calendar of the Soul* in 1912, we can find a golden thread linking the various ways Scorpio acts as a constant blueprint in nature.

Description of the glyph

Three descending movements, like commas, with the fourth moving up like an arrow: they may be emphasizing the functional threefoldedness of all living creatures (head—neural function, thorax—rhythm and abdomen—transformation of substances). A further threefoldedness can be found in the body nesting the soul that nests the spirit. The arrow shows an individual hereditary direction of a threefoldedness in space.

There is a dual archetype in the conventional picture: scorpion and eagle. On one side a terrestrial nocturnal creature and on the other side an aerial diurnal creature living on mountain peaks 'where its flight can overview the landscape'.[2]

Description of the Drawing

In Imma's drawing we see a set of primitive forms within a vertical framework, and can observe at the centre a white egg shape capped by a circle. This is defined by a darker surrounding pressing in and delineating it. The circle radiates upwards towards the periphery. The egg shape is surrounded on both sides by five long rays alternating between dark and light.

Towards the centre of the egg we have two human heads. One is the profile of a young man with short black hair looking to the right, fused with a young female face with long, light curly hair looking at us. Two strong lines descend from the neck of each head to the bottom periphery of the egg expressing a unity of construction inside the egg.

Above these heads, standing in the circle, there are simplified outlines suggesting two sleepy eyes and a nose, with a strong horizontal curvy movement just above.

If we look at the relation of the egg to the circle we notice that the circle is an irradiating sun that seems to press down on top of the egg as if a formative impulse is penetrating the egg. There is definitely a descending direction expressed here. The lines that suggest eyes and nose infer a state of sleepiness, the dormancy of an embryo in development.

What is there just at the centre of the egg? Is it a suggestion of Janus, the two-headed Roman god?

The origin of the name Janus is disputed among etymologists, who say it's from an Indo-European language, as well as Greek and Latin. It includes the notion of fertile chaos where form, substance and breath are mingled together undifferentiated, a bit like a butterfly cocoon. It also has the flavour of a beginning or transition where chaos is always present. Janus also means the bright light of the sun.[3]

These disputed interpretations of the word Janus can be observed in this drawing. We have the bright light of the sun (circle) entering the embryo-like suggested form (egg) marking the beginning of a transition. The whole fertile chaos of the development of an embryo where organs appear and disappear, or change location in the forming of an organism is suggested.

However, the Janus of the drawing has one head looking sideways and the other looking at us directly. They are young figures as opposed to the traditional representation which is of two bearded old men looking in opposite directions. With the two strong lines descending from their necks they seem to have an influence on a territory inside the egg.

'But in winter soul-spiritual activities resume with renewed forces. Around Christmas and the New Year, at the beginning of January [Janus], the soul activity in liver and kidneys reaches its culmination. The Romans knew this, and that's why they call this two-faced being, the January being.'[4]

What is the essence of the kidneys and liver?

The kidneys have the shape of kidney beans. The kidneys continually contract the blood stream by bringing its mineral and organic constituents into an ideal concentration for a spirit to incarnate. Every second of our life they dose the liquid tissue (blood) to an ideal composition by getting rid of any unessential substances (urine). Recovering its essence with the kidneys, the blood flows in the intimacy of each organ. This is the physiological basis for our health, consequently allowing the talent-potential of an incarnate spirit to achieve its destiny.

The liver, as a plant-like organ, expands the blood stream with fresh new substances to a degree favourable for the germination of a territory and its defence. These two activities work in all embryos even before the organs appear and still work at the adult stage. The profile face in the drawing has more contracted features — the one facing us is more expansive.

What about this strange curvy line, coiling up the horizontal in the circle? From the left to the centre, then to the right we have a strange movement. This can be seen as two wavy lines coming from opposite directions and ending in a sharp sting shape resembling the deadly tail of a scorpion. It represents two streams of energy, like cold dry air meeting warm damp air, creating a vortical twister. Whatever we see in these lines, they suggest an agitation carrying influences that are not necessarily comfortable.

Carbon: a Shaper of Structure

'Carbon made the earth a planet bearing the plants and all pro-cesses of structuration [construction], of densification.'[5]

When carbon is associated with oxygen and hydrogen, it cre-ates a vegetal architecture (carbohydrate). When we add nitro-gen to these three we end up with a protein architecture that allows animal and human constitutions. Carbon, with its four valences, tends in nature to associate only with hydrogen, oxy-gen, nitrogen and itself (e.g. diamond), forming several million types of compounds. It helps to create the scaffold-like structure for all forms of living matter. It is a shaper of molecular structure generating chains, rings, etc. and organizing the basic framework of organic substances. There is no embryonic development without this form-giving element.

There is a lot to say about carbon in nature. The plants extract it from carbon dioxide in the air during photosynthesis. From its pure crystal (diamond) form, one of the hardest substances known, to its man-made monolayered crystal hexagonal form (graphene), with strange semiconductive properties to transfer information (heat and electricity), we have a substance that has many faces.

Amphibian: the Beginning of Terrestrial Vertebrates

Amphibian—frog, salamander: 2,500 species

Scorpio is a leap impulse. This can happen only at the embryonic level where there is genetic plasticity. The ocean is absolutely packed with embryonic seeds from invertebrate phyla. We saw with the pro-chordata tunicata (Aries impulse) an embryonic stage that opened the door for the vertebrate expression. Some of these living embryos are still there in the ocean today (lancelet).

Each phylum is a new beginning, a moment of transition moving towards a new step in complexity and consciousness. Sudden evolutionary leaps can happen very fast, judging by the geological fossil record. From what we know the earth's surface has moved quite a lot during the aeons of its existence through tectonic plate movements. The fossil record shows major and minor periods of extinction due to the earth's drastic changes and outside agency (meteorite or even asteroid impacts). The earth's crust moves sideways but also up and down. What geobiologists often don't mention is the fact that these extinction events are always accompanied by new creations, always manifesting more complex forms and instincts.

Before the dinosaurs, and paving the way towards them, another major leap occurred. The passage from living in water to living in the air required such a leap. From water to air we increase our weight by a factor of hundred. This presents quite a structural challenge. It demands a completely different body organization in order to cope with gravity and extract oxygen from the air. The first vertebrates to tackle the problem were the amphibians (frogs, salamanders). In those days plants and insects were well on their way to populate air and solid ground. From a fish-like embryonic state during the primary period (tadpole), this phylum emerged tentatively on the shores of the continents and keeps, to this day, a strong link with water and damp conditions for survival. Though they do have primitive lungs they breathe more through their damp skin than their nose.

There is something like an embryo even in the adults of this animal group. Change in the genome of a species will never come from a specialized well-developed adult. Several species of amphibian live their lives at different stages of embryonic development and keep their tadpole shape (e.g. some newts). Amphibians still rely on water for their egg production, and create a great abundance of eggs and larva.

The adults of this group are expressing, for the first time, four limbs with five extensions at their ends. These five finger-like expressions can be seen in the drawing around the outside of the egg shape parting the dark area. They tend to crawl on earth and due to their powerful thighs (Sagittarius influence) they jump fast and far. The frogs use their limbs and fingers to row their way on the surface of the ground or paddle in water.

Here there is not only a sense of smell but also the development of proper ears. Frogs can also produce sound and excrete a lymph-like fluid on the skin that is sometimes poisonous in tropical countries.

The sense of smell

Even though they can breathe through their sensitive skins, amphibians do have rudimentary lungs that seem to appear in tandem with the extensions of the limbs. As they are creatures now living in the air rather than water the sense of smell also appears in the vertebrates for the first time. Insects must also have some sense of smell in their abdominal breathing systems, and they have very sensitive antennae making them aware of all sorts of influences present in the air. But amphibians develop smell for the first time as land-dwelling vertebrates. Sea animals taste and smell at the same time with their skin and gills which is quite a different process.

All smells are in a gaseous state. It is a subtle emanation of things. Because living creatures emit various and volatile hydrogen compounds (essential oils), they fill the air with their emanations. Like all gases, these essences expand in the air, create pressure on the solid state and penetrate water and organic membranes. We shouldn't underestimate the formative power of smell for our internal organs, as well as for our psychic activity. A small area of our nose makes us aware of a small range of these emanations. Animals are much better at it. Our taste buds can register only five or six flavours, but our capacity to differentiate aromas seems infinite.

The Creation of Genetic Uniqueness

The metabolic process of the moon sphere is reproduction by mitosis, which is what all our cells perform when they divide. By doing so they end up with an identical set of chromosomes (cloning). The curvy line above the sleepy eyes in Imma's drawing represents a new form of transmission of genetic material where two ancestral streams are involved. It is the meiotic process where two parents give only half of their genetic material. Then we end up with individuals carrying a unique chromosomal configuration that will never happen again. Because of this Scorpio has the sting of death. The phenomenon of the birth process is linked with the death process when two streams of parents are involved: everything is transitory. The genetic make-up from two parents is unique and will never happen again. Many invertebrates have both the budding-cloning process of reproduction and the meiotic one. Others, such as the earthworm and octopus, are hermaphroditic (the individual holds the two halves), but still need a stimulating partner during the period of reproduction.

Progressively we have sexual differentiation with specific organs for the meiotic event. Already in fishes and frogs, who rely on water to mate, many species have a tendency to protect the eggs.

Mars Sphere Rules Scorpio

Already mentioned with Aries, Mars has the pulsing breath of a warrior around the grey matter of the brain essential for consciousness to grasp the perception preserved in the nerves. There is no image of a sensation in our consciousness without this pulsing breathing rhythm around the grey cells where the blood flow meets the nerve current.

When we want to build a house we take nature's creation (trees, rocks) into a new architecture. It involves transformation. The gall bladder, with its concentrated bile helps enzymes to transform food. In both cases it is a matter of dismembering one thing (Mars activity) to create another.

Consonant S

With this sound the sphincter muscle around the lips is very active. The teeth must meet correctly. The tongue flattens in the mouth.

'In the muscles of the lower lip [and mobile jaw] we have an intense concentration of our karma.'[6]

'S leads the soul into matter.' It 'is the consonant of consonants, the sound that penetrates deepest into matter and forms S'.[7]

Conclusion

Meiotic division started very early in invertebrates. It allowed the potential of a species' genome to express itself more fully. The genome is the sum total of the genes carried by the chromosomes of the races of a species. Cats and dogs were domesticated a long time ago; the various races we have today didn't exist in the wild. By crossbreeding them man was able to explore the full gamut of expression hidden in the chromosomes of these species.

For us, heredity is a vast topic. In ancient Chinese physiology, the word 'heredity' included the moment of conception, the nine months in the mother, the moment of birth and the early years. This is the basis of our cultural heredity. The Chinese acknowledged that the mother, the family and the cultural input bring major imprints in the newborn baby.

They were also aware of a creative spirit (*Shen*) offering its own talents and potential. Heredity also included the genetic aspect where two ancestral streams unite to give the basic genes/chromosomes to create a child. This, of course, comes with strengths and weaknesses of organ systems. In the Old Testament and in homoeopathy they say that we bear the sins of our parents for seven generations.

From one phylum to another there is always a huge structural leap with a new instinctual behaviour. Instinct and its animal form can't be separated. An embryo evolves through growth and is in constant metamorphosis. It is matter in motion going in a specific direction of expression that can't be changed. This direction is under the governance of an entelechy, meaning a certain state of perfection within, whatever its stage of development. It refers to a soul/spirit entity of some kind able to direct its progress in order for a potential to become a physical actuality.

An inner cage is created in the thorax for the lung and heat (inner movement) at the same time that the limbs express themselves (outer movement). Whenever there is a metamorphosis there is always a tendency for balance to be produced between outer and inner expression. Goethe called this law 'the law of balancing the sheet'.[8]

The sharp sting above the eyes in Imma's drawing is in the pineal gland area (sixth chakra or third eye) that can influence the instinctual activity of reproduction through its melatonin secretion. Instinct for each species is a set of behaviours which doesn't require cognitive consciousness. It is an inborn inclination where complex patterns of activity rule survival, reproduction, food intake, etc. Whatever instinct appears in nature, it starts in an embryo.

Carbon gives physical form to all living matter. All living beings live with a scaffold-like skeleton (cellulose for plant cells or proteinic fibres for animal cells). And a skeleton is the hardened version of the individuality. No two human skeletons are the same.

Carbon as a structural element is part of the atmospheric cross, also called the organic cross. We have hydrogen (Leo) with its opposite oxygen (Aquarius) and nitrogen (Taurus) with its opposite carbon (Scorpio). These four elements form the basis of the air we breathe as well as the basis of the organic world.[9]

Atmospheric or the organic cross

Taurus (nitrogen)

Aquarius (oxygen)   Leo (hydrogen)

Scorpio (carbon)

10. Libra

Preamble

Being alive is a knife-edge experience all the time tending towards fulcrum points suitable for the emergence and health of living organisms. Even the earth, be it the salinity of water or the atmospheric composition among so many parameters, has developed complex systems of regulation that maintain the right balance of compounds for the manifestation of life. It has always been a fragile equilibrium between Ice Ages and tropical periods. Periods of contraction like night or winter, and periods of expansion like day and summer, are part of this constant recycling of the states of matter. Everything is on the move but is it all just random activity?

In the earth as a whole, as well as inside any living species, there is a tendency to maintain constant the basic parameters for manifest life: this is called homeostasis. Life is a fragile rhythmic balance. James Lovelock, in his book *Gaia*, invited different disciplines to work together to try to understand how the earth has maintained its dynamic consistency over the aeons.

Like any other concepts we can always add content to the 'word or thought biosphere'. We can imagine a sphere of activity around the earth in air, water and solid ground where we perceive the living and material kingdoms in action.

James Hutton, the Scottish founder of geology in the eighteenth century, saw the earth as a super-organism on the move where the mineral and living kingdoms interact with one another as a self-regulatory entity. We live in mountains made by the constant sedimentation of living organisms at the bottom of the sea. Coupled with earth actions that compress the sediments in an incessant up/down movement and we have the ground we walk on. Petrol comes from living activity when the earth was younger and tropical. The concept of biosphere includes this constant co-evolution of the three kingdoms interpenetrating one another.

Mankind is the fourth kingdom and our civilizations live inside ecosystems that they transform too. With the technical advances of the last century, man's capacity to manipulate and destroy nature has increased exponentially. Rooted in ecosystems, if we damage nature, we damage the nest.

Life has deeply changed the mineral kingdom over aeons. This text introduces another super-sensible dimension to this concept of the biosphere: the influx of subtle formative forces from the stars giving orientation to the Life project.

Nevertheless the emergence and maintenance of forms is still a total mystery. It is not because we know the architects (formative forces) of a building or even its builders of all trades (elemental tradesmen) that we know the one (spirit) who had the intention to build it.

Inside us the same knife-edge path is ever present. We live within a narrow range of heat (around 98 F or 37 C) or a specific

The Constellation of Libra (The Scales)

amount of sugar in the blood stream (90mg per 100 ml of blood).[1]
A little bit above or below these fulcrum points and our physical
and mental health loses its ground very quickly. Minute quantities of organic (hormones) and inorganic substances (potassium, sodium, copper, manganese, cobalt, calcium, etc.) all work
at a fulcrum point.

Introduction

This text explores the imprint of the intelligent action of Libra all
around us in the constant forming of human and animal creation.
What is the relation between the Libra sector of space, its glyph,
the medieval image of this constellation, Imma's drawing, the
element calcium, the animal phylum reptile, the sense of balance,
the hip, Venus as a ruling planet, the colour gentian-violet and
the consonant TZ? Based on Imma's drawings in the first edition
of *The Calendar of the Soul* in 1912, we can find a golden thread
linking the various ways Libra acts as a constant blueprint in
nature.

Description of the Glyph

The Libra glyph consists of a horizontal line with another one on
top that has a bulge or half circle in the middle. This suggests an
activity that strives towards a fulcrum point. The traditional
picture shows a man with his two hands holding a pair of scales
and focused on stabilizing it at its point of equilibrium.

Description of the Drawing

At first glance this drawing shows a structural solidity. It is a
balanced set of vertical and horizontal lines. The top third is
lighter with a central circle or sphere, emitting rays from dif-

ferent directions of space. This circle is porous and extends two arms horizontally, while a vertical beam goes behind the sphere parting the top drawing into two equal sectors. The circle is at a fulcrum point.

Then a thick horizontal beam which looks like wood holds the light part of the drawing from the darker lower part and supports the irradiating globe. It looks like a clear division between the spiritual and the material. The top part looks much lighter, whereas the bottom part has density. The boundary between the two zones is interactive, asking the question: Is the white top pressing down or is the black bottom holding it up?

Just below the wooden beam is an area filled with darkness that scintillates with clear dots. In the middle of this black area there is an inverted egg shape with a black cross in the middle. The cross is surrounded in the egg by smoke and flame irradiating from the bottom of the cross as if it is in a process of disintegration. The black vertical is slightly out of phase with the white one but does run from top to bottom of the egg while the horizontal part of the cross doesn't touch the edge of the egg and forms a fulcrum with the vertical part.

The egg seems to be in a precarious position standing on its tip. It looks as if a pressure works downwards from the top lighter area and imposes its weight on the black cross, provoking the burning of the bottom part of the egg. The whole egg interior seems pretty hot with smoke. No movement here, just a fragile equilibrium. The cross is a symbol of man crucified in matter: the vertical descent from the spirit world into the horizontal realm of matter.

Calcium: A Substance for Solidity and Movement

Many phyla use calcium as an external protection (e.g. snail). Their sediment has helped to form mountain ranges. The oceans owe their clarity partially to them. There is something of a dry structure about this drawing and also about calcium—no colloidal lime. Calcium is inclined to aridity and doesn't relate well with water. Nevertheless calcium is essential for bone firmness in the creation of our skeletons (99 per cent). Its presence in small quantities in our extracellular liquid is essential for muscle contraction (conscious movement), bioelectric impulse of the nerves (sensory-motor activity) and blood coagulation (scarring – immunity).

It is also essential for chromosomal movement (unconscious) in cellular division, the formation of glycogen (muscle fuel), as well as the synthesis and liberation of neurotransmitters for nervous influx. The fulcrum of this substance in the blood is regulated by two hormones from the larynx area: calcitonin and parathormone. The fulcrum point is 4.3 to 5.3 mEq of calcium per litre of blood. (mEq = milliequivalent).[2] Calcium also acts as an acidity buffer in the blood to maintain a pH just above 7. How all the fulcrum points are determined remains mysterious.

Reptiles: The Armoured Ones Conquer the Solid Ground

Reptiles – snake, crocodile, turtle, lizard: c. 6,000 species
The first vertebrate phyla that really manage to achieve mastery over gravity on land are the reptiles with their scaly skin. The amphibia started a semi-aquatic existence with a skeleton allowing them to crawl, hop or jump on the earth. With the reptiles a new mastery of the skeleton is achieved. The articulation of the vertebral column with the lower limbs allows a better distribution of weight. Thanks to the sacrum/hip the weight is transferred evenly to the feet, allowing greater speed, agility and mobility in the lizard group. Some of them will even dare to erect to a vertical position (Tyrannosaurus rex). Like the mammalian kangaroo, the vertical reptilian giants had to grow enormous tails for balance, while keeping short front limbs.

It is interesting to observe that during the reptilian expression the amphibians nearly disappear from the map. The geological fossil record shows vast extinctions. There must have been some pockets of resistance, because after the reptilian extinction (65 million years ago), amphibians reappeared in great numbers. So it is for the mammals (rodent or meerkat-like creatures) living under the floor of vast tropical forests. They couldn't express their varieties under the reign of the reptiles. Because of these ferocious armed beasts, the amphibia and mammals didn't have a chance. The reptile conquered solid earth (dinosaurs), the oceans (plesiosaurs) and even attempted to invade the air (pterosaurs).

With the reptiles we have the beginning of hard calcium egg-shells protecting embryos. Here is the start of internalized reproduction. Fertilization in primitive phyla occurs in water (except for some classes of insects and annelids) and the eggs are left to the elements. Reptiles were the first vertebrates to have internal fertilization accompanied by a calcium-based shell surrounding the embryo (oviparous) like a kind of portable uterus.

Why this egg shape? Maybe these specific curves on the egg, based on the mathematic concept of infinity, are aerials picking up influences from the super-sensible realm (formative forces).

We already know a specific aerial shape is needed to capture electromagnetic radiations (sub-sensible forces) so why not aerials for super-sensible forces? Each species of reptile and bird develops its specific egg curve. Some reptiles even start to hatch their young inside (ovoviviparous).

Sense of Balance

A child will take about three years to master his vertical position against gravity. This is the equivalent of a university degree. In order to do this he will progressively synchronize his sense of balance in the inner ear with the whole bone-muscle system. Conquering gravity on a daily basis is a constant effort but we don't notice the muscles involved. Learned in childhood it becomes a lifelong reflex. The sense of balance makes us conscious that our weight is attracted towards the centre of the earth, anchoring us to the solid state of matter.

A Structure to Live with Gravity: Hips

The frog tribe coming out of the liquid element can crawl or leap with their powerful thighs. Their hips coordinate the back limbs with the front ones. It is with the reptile family that the hips start to be more mobile and flexible to conquer the earth. These scaly-skinned animals have much more mobility on the ground. Tyrannosaurus rex is the first creature to walk on two legs. With the mammals the kangaroos will try the same thing, ending up with two little arms and long tail also used for balance. The sacrum transfers the weight of the upper body to two legs with the help of the hips.

Venus Sphere Rules Libra

The Venus metabolic process has to do with harmonious growth and regeneration, the constant renewal of our organs. This is the function of the kidneys, the Venus organ.

Kidney activity gives a ratio of mineral and organic substances vital to harmonious growth. This activity can take place without the organ in primitive animals, just as the circulation in the primitive embryo doesn't need the physical heart. It brings the internal liquids at a proper level of dilution (contraction) for an intelligent activity to embed in matter.

Venus's metal is copper and, like all metals, it is a congealed flowing force. It produces colours in both the mineral and the living realm.

'... for the various ores have a shining splendour that ranges from blue and green to red and purple. [...] Few substances possess such a beauty.'[3]

Copper, like some other ores has a special affinity to water.

'We may say, then, that copper absorbs water and changes it into form and colour.'[3]

It is not surprising that so many animals, including the invertebrates, use copper for their external colourful appearance. Copper is also used as a breathing pigment by many invertebrates to capture oxygen, and is an essential enzymatic co-factor in the formation of our haemoglobin red pigment in the blood.

The liver has the biggest concentration of copper as a reserve. We can find copper in the substantia nigra of the brain responsible for the production of the pigment melanin. In so many ways copper has to do with pigment.

Copper is also an essential micro-element for the efficient use of the B vitamin group (another enzymatic co-factor). Both are activators of the growing process.

Consonant: Tz

Tz is the sound we make when we sneeze, in an attempt to recover an inner balance in our rhythmic system.

The fingers of the two hands gently hit the top of the head in the eurythmy gesture for the consonant T. It is a kind of invitation for the spirit to penetrate more deeply into the soul.

According to Steiner, it is a sound of health that harmonizes a temporary disharmony between the heartbeat and breathing. It is very good for the heart to sneeze out loud, helping to overcome the initial resistance of the soul to be penetrated by the spirit.[4]

Steiner merely says it is the sound of health.[5]

Conclusion

Achieving balance between pairs of opposites has been a constant challenge for life on earth. Growth and health are only possible with a multitude of fulcrum-like points. How do these fulcrum points emerge as the best scenario for life?

Libra brings homeostasis, a knife-edge experience, in living systems. It is a kind of dynamic, structural, hormonal, etc. equilibrium that must be maintained at all cost.

The sacrum/hips are the basic bone structure for incarnated vertebrates confronted with the terrestrial force of gravity. From this bone structure the reptile gains a greater mobility (e.g. lizard).

Calcium is a white soft metal, part of the mineral cross (or cardinal cross) in the zodiac. In its pure form it is a transparent crystal (calcite). With the four minerals — calcium (Libra) opposing silica (Aries) and phosphorus (Cancer) opposing aluminium (Capricorn) in the zodiac wheel — we have the basis of our solid earth (geosphere).[6]

Geosphere or the basic elements of the solid earth (mineral cross)[7]

Cancer (phosphorus)

Aries (silica)   Libra (calcium)

Capricorn (aluminium)

11. Virgo

Preamble

'Matter is a heap of ruins of the spirit, ... scattered spirit. It is extraordinarily important to grasp this definition.'[1]

There are conscious presences around us all the time. All the four kingdoms of nature have intelligence to various degrees.

'If a spirit breaks into the void (the virgin soil) then mineral matter results.'[1]

Mineral matter has three states (solid, liquid and gas) with a fourth that is not recognized in modern science as a state: heat. Nevertheless, scientists acknowledge a very hot start for the universe. By fragmenting matter to its ultimate particles, they reach a very high temperature in the Hadron Collider.

Steiner called the primeval heat of the solar system 'Old Saturn' in his book *Occult Science*. It is not easy to imagine a world made only of heat but the spirits of the different kingdoms, in their descent into density, come from infinitely hot spirit realms. It is through a progressive cooling that the 92 elements of the mineral kingdom emerge in their three states in the furnace of the stars.

At a certain point the conditions on earth were perfect to allow water to experience its three states in a harmonious way under the guidance of heat. Contraction and expansion are the features of the etheric realm bordering the physical. Water expands and contracts all the time. When earthly conditions are favourable and there is an availability of flowing water, an etheric and physical form is possible. If a spirit meets this, 'when this is the case, plant matter originates'.[1]

Plants transform the air around the earth by bringing free oxygen and aromas. This allows a new kind of creature that can perceive the world (sensorial organs) and move into it (muscles).

A connection between these two is needed to link perception with movement, allowing a conscious presence to be 'in' nature: this is the material nerve substance. Then a spirit has the power to generate a proteinic architecture (animal) bringing organs (astral body coupled with an etheric body) that reflect the activity of the planetary spheres.

The spirit of each species of plants has a physical body emerging out of an etheric organization that produces a carbohydrate architecture.

The spirit of each species of animal has also an etheric building force like the plants but nested inside an astral vehicle that allows a proteinic architecture. It is called astral because this subtle vehicle provides the morphic field for organs under the influence of the seven planetary spheres.

These proteinic organs, in the course of evolution, will allow more conscious psychic activity (instinctive behaviour) for the incarnated animal soul-group. Human beings, formed in the same way, reach a level of self-consciousness where the soul faculties (thinking, feeling, willing) can be used by the spirit to overcome animality. Each human being is a species by himself.

It is in this spirit's descent into matter, from the supra-earthly to the sensible world, that other sub-earthly forces are generated as shadows (e. g. electricity, magnetism). Our own nerves produce a bioelectric influx, and the heart has a larger magnetic field than the brain's. We also, of course, live in the vast electric and magnetic fields of the earth.

A description of this mysterious material manifestation of nature is given by Goethe in *An Essay in Aphorisms on Nature*:

'Nature! We are surrounded and enveloped by her — unable to step out of her, unable to get into her more deeply. Unasked and unwarned, she takes us up into the circle of her dance and carries us along till we are wearied and fall from her arms.' And so on for a few pages — a highly recommended three pages.

Because of our recent mastery of these sub-forces (such as electromagnetism), mankind has filled the air with frequencies (e.g. radio, microwave) for communication purposes. Around us the air is chock-a-block with sounds and images coming from various frequency sources. We access these if we have the right apparatus (transducers such as radios, TVs or mobile phones). If this world of electromagnetic radiations is a shadow of the supra-earthly working on the sensible world, then the space around us must be filled also with thought forms from the supra-earthly realm. In this super-sensible realm a thought form/being/vector of intelligent activity/deity/formative force are all the same thing. We are densely surrounded by these coming from all sectors of space. How can we access them? The brain is our transducer but, like any radio system that receives multiple frequencies, we have to tune it. There is an intention to listen here.

'Thanks to our brain we can utilize for our own benefit the intelligence in all things.'[2]

Adam and Eve bit an apple and incarnated into the sensible realm. The logo for the technology company Apple Inc. is an apple with a bite out of it. When we are at the computer we are in the sub-world (infra-earthly), a virtual world below the sensible. This technology is a fantastic tool, but, like any technology, it brings challenges at various levels for the life processes in us.

One of these challenges is the fact that in the last few decades we have enormously increased radio and microwave frequencies for the purpose of transmission of information (millions of times higher than the background cosmic frequencies). These frequencies pulse at a low rate close to the multiple pulsations of living creatures. We need to be careful not to overexpose ourselves to the pulsed radiation that can disturb our own pulses. Cases of hypersensitivity are on the increase.

With this interactive technology (the Internet) it is easy to suffer from a kind of image bulimia. How can we digest all these images and all this information? The medium itself tends to destroy inner silence. This means a decrease of inner perception (insight). It may also be detrimental for human relationships, removing us from real people. Each person has to make his or her own decision on how to relate with it.

Constellation of Virgo (The Virgin)

Content

This text explores the imprint of the intelligent activity of Virgo all around us in the constant forming of human and animal creation. What is the relation between the Virgo sector of space, its glyph, the medieval image of this constellation, Imma's drawing, the element sodium, the animal phylum birds, the movement sense, the belly, earth as a ruling planet, the colour indigo and the consonants B, P? Based on Imma's drawings in the first edition of *The Calendar of the Soul* in 1912, we can try to find a golden thread linking the various ways Virgo acts as a constant blueprint in nature.

Description of the Glyph and Traditional Picture

As with Scorpio, there are three arm-like gestures a bit like the letter M, with a fourth that returns and crosses the last one. This triune movement of the glyph is a symbol of the three states of matter (solid, liquid, gas) ruled by the fourth state (heat) that turns its tail towards the other three and acts as a maestro of ceremonies. Heat determines these states of matter, whether something is solid, liquid or gas.

The traditional picture shows a woman holding corn or a baby, both symbols of fertility and nurturing. As the largest of the twelve constellations in the Milky Way, Virgo holds the mystery of matter and its three states are constantly informed by heat.

Description of the Drawing

Imma's drawing has gravitas but also radiates levity. A woman stands inside and dominates the drawing. Covered with a flowing garment, she is holding a child. Like the Scorpio and Libra drawings, the central image is inside an egg shape capped by a circle. The child holds a black globe with a cross on top. The porous circle above shows the head of the lady in a globe where rays shine out.

The woman's neck has a collar made of three rings plus three lines below (trinity or three in one). Her head is crowned with seven flat vertical elements.

'Three has a structuring and organizing quality.'[3]

It has been named The Queen of Numbers.[4] The three collars and lines may be interpreted as the threefold centres of man— head, thorax and abdomen, or the root, leaf and flower of the plant kingdom. It can also be seen as the mineral kingdom with its solid, liquid and gas states, according to the amount of heat in them.

The seven crown slats may refer to so many things. Seven is 'the number of time'[5] and transformation. The seven slats may be the seven days of the week that relate with the seven planetary spheres looping around the earth, reverberating in us as the seven metabolic activities. The seven chakras that interface the soul (three faculties) can also be included here.

The egg shape is surrounded on each side by five feather-like structures like the teeth of a saw. The white ones radiate outward and mingle with the dark ones that ray inward. A crescent moon sits at the bottom of the mantle as a cradle for the profile of a man's head looking up. A child rests in the mother's mantle.

The face of the woman is not delineated even if we have suggested eyes, brows, nose and mouth. Her eyes look sideways and her face is grave with a look of suspicious anticipation. The child seems ready to go out of the nest with one leg out, but a hand of the mother is holding him. The child is looking at us.

The most ancient name for Virgo's formative force is Lilith. Periods of pre-historical human society are thought to have been matriarchal and honoured Lilith before the current patriarchal age. For some Kabbalists of the Jewish tradition, Lilith corresponds to Malkuth, the sensible realm (material kingdom) where Virgo orients matter into three states (solid, liquid and gas) with a metamorphic state (heat). Lilith means: the one who brings bright wind where all the diverse energies flow.[6]

In this descent, matter is accompanied by elemental spirits. In this dual world of male-female or North-South Magnetic Poles, each material state is coupled with an intelligent activity (elemental spirits living in the realm bordering the physical). In the past humans had more communion with the moving flow of natural beings acting behind the perceptible world, and this communion was more intense during a matriarchal time (e.g. Crete).

These subtle elemental forces (four ethers) essentially keep matter in movement. They don't generate the form but they build it. They are the last etheric workers bringing the forms of the living kingdoms into existence, following the design of the formative forces (planets for internal organs with their metabolic processes and constellations for the external shape or form). In the past these elemental forces could be handled by humans for healing (white magic) or in egoistic ways (black magic). That is why Lilith is also later associated with demons. Natural forces become malignant when used for greed.

Virgo is also Ishtar, the eight-pointed star symbol of the Babylonians, meaning the light bringer through procreation allowing fertility, love, motherhood, the use of magic by mankind and warfare.[7] Oh, really? Warfare? It is a simple historical fact that at the edges of any empire or civilization there have always been barbarians both in times of war and peace. So it is for our individual empire (our body). Here we have permanent warfare waged by our immune system. The constant invasion of bacteria, viruses, etc. must be kept at bay. We live in symbiosis with them but they also have to stay at the edge of our empire. They are useful to digest dead skin and in the large intestine to complete digestion, but they are stopped at these boundaries lest they create havoc inside us. The physical life of all species is in a state of permanent symbiosis and warfare with these little creatures.

Virgo is also Isis, and the child Horus, in ancient Egypt. They became Mary and the infant Jesus in our modern Christian era.

The Great Mother in the drawing has a profile of an old man at her feet inside a crescent moon. Is it Janus looking sideways? For the ancient Romans Janus, the two-headed god, was the guardian of the gates of the city (every Roman town had one). This god's activity registered people and goods coming in and out. By memorizing past events as well as their future implications, the city could have a better grip on its present. In the drawing Janus is a symbol of the record of events. In this face is an immobile active listener, the feminine aspect of Janus's role. The whole content of the evolutionary process is never forgotten. It is written somewhere in the ether (universal consciousness) or what the ancient Sanskrit language calls the Akashic record.

Most civilizations do their best to record their history and ours, using the forces of electricity and magnetism, excels as far as recording/transmitting is concerned—it's dazzling. The computing phenomenon is just a shadow reflection of what happens at a higher level. The Akasha is the record in the ether of human and cosmic activities. We have our way and nature has hers. Janus in Imma's drawing is a reminder of the fact that nothing goes to oblivion. The moon reflects the sun and Janus's face rests there recording natural and human events on earth.

The baby represents the physical entry of a human being on earth with a self-conscious individual spirit. In the Christian tradition, it is the Christ-child figure inviting us to master the soul/body animality, opening the possibility to reconnect with the spiritual, in freedom. Each human with its self-consciousness is a unique seed or species that has a creative spirit wanting to flourish and manifest its destiny. If this 'I am' takes hold of his vast amount of instinctual behaviour, or this polymorphous web of urges, desires, then his body/soul can start to lift back to the spiritual while living on earth. Only the 'I am' can overcome this duality and find levity on its way back to the spiritual.

Sodium: an Agitated Colloidal Element

Table salt is a mineralized balance between a base (Na-alkali) and an acid forming force (Cl-halogen). Alkalis, like sodium (Na), are prone to a colloidal state.

'Often they dissolve slowly into a colloidal system, particularly in the presence of "protective colloids" such as proteins.'[8]

'Alkalis, then, have a proclivity to form enclosing sheaths, and the colloidal state may be looked upon as a further development in this direction.'[9]

This is another common denominator between all living species: the colloidal state coupled with the right amount of salt.

'All the up-build processes, having to do with growth and nutrition in plants, animals and humans alike, are maintained by alkaline colloids present in the fluids of the various organs. In plants this alkali is chiefly potassium; in men and animals, sodium.'[10]

Sodium and chlorine are polar opposites in terms of their properties. Chlorine is an acid-forming entity that tends to dissolve the colloidal sodium state. Their interaction creates a third force: the salt of the earth so essential for life.

If one searches for an appropriate picture to express artistically the nature of alkali's enclosing gesture, we come upon the pictures of a maternal organism giving shelter to the child-to-be. She has wrapped her mantle protectively around it. We feel in the gesture her connection with the heavenly powers for which she has provided earthly shelter. In ancient times, when no one doubted that the terrestrial is always a housing for the spirit, this truth was felt to be pictured in the constellation of Virgo, the virgin. Here could be experienced the sheath-forming power, whence forces of fertility and ripening rayed down to earth.[11]

Birds: The Conquest of the Air

Birds: c. 8,600 species

The space around the egg in the drawing holds some feather-like structures that give it levity. Birds fly between gravity and levity.

The first vertebrates to populate the air are the birds. They appear at the end of the dinosaur era. They kept many characteristics of the reptile phylum, with an impetus to conquer the air and travel all over the globe in migratory north/south tracts. The bird walks on two legs, freeing the upper limbs to fly. Feathers keep the body dry and warm (the word duvet is the name given to feathers close to the body).

Isis, another name for the Great Mother nurturing a child (Horus), is often shown with a row of feathers on her opened arms. Like the mammal phylum, birds are warm-blooded. The hollow of their bones acts like a lung, giving them more levity. They also tend their young with great attention and warmth in the most ingenious ways (mouth-to-mouth feeding). Having conquered the air they also fill it with myriad sounds with their double larynx/syrinx.

As in each phylum, different species explore different aspects of the inherent threefoldness in the kingdoms of nature (head/neuro-sensorial, thorax/rhythmic and abdomen/metabolic). By their physical shape some show a more pronounced metabolic process (goose). With the eagle, living high up in the mountains, the head/neuro-sensorial complex predominates. A multitude of others live more in the rhythmic/thorax area and are very colourful and musical.

The Sense of Movement

Each phylum generates its own way of moving in water or air. With the birds we reach a peak of expression where gravity doesn't seem to exist anymore.

'Birds have a marvellously developed sense of motion, a feeling for their own movement, especially in the chest region where the wings originate. The breast muscles are most power-ful. Their capacity for movement is enormous with great sensi-tivity to the atmospheric currents.'[12]

We have all admired the choreography of hundreds of birds (starlings) playing in the air as one soul-group.

Primal Nourishing Milk Invites a New Incarnation

Tradition places the Virgo formative force in the belly area. This force has to do with the solar plexus that rules the process of assimilation through the sympathetic nervous system. When we are born we need our mothers' milk. Later we digest food to make our own milk (intestinal chyme). The solar system is nested in a galaxy (the Milky Way) that is constantly sending the nourishing subtle influences of the constellations amplified by the sun.

The lower belly area, with the uterus, offers a space for new incarnation where the mother nourishes the embryo/foetus.

Planet Earth rules Virgo

On earth the four states of matter interplay in such a way that life's rhythms allow spirit to evolve and produce unconscious (mineral and plant), conscious (animal) and self-conscious beings (human).

Consonant: B, P

The sounds B and P start by a contraction of abdominal muscles accompanied by a compressing of the lips. This process builds up a pressure of air in the mouth and then the B or P can explode.

'When the force of B comes, then part of the spirit (baby) is separated from the whole and enclosed in the individual womb as a flower bud is separated from the outside, whereas P in contrast stands for the embracing protecting quality of the mother.'[13]

'Their formative power [sound] works in the activity of the solar plexus, the mysterious sun centre which oversees the process of assimilation and of the sympathetic system.'[14]

Conclusion

From counterspace spirits come first into the void (virgin soil) and then matter arises. Virgo's activity orients matter's expression towards three states in constant metamorphosis through a master of ceremonies: heat. The formative forces of Virgo are not Gaia but provide the material garment for her. Gaia is the name given to the whole earth as a living goddess, with its various inner and outer layers, by the ancient Greeks. Whereas the Demeter/Persephone Greek myth reflects more the expression of the perpetual spring-summer return of life on the surface of the earth (biosphere).

'The eternal feminine draws us forwards' appears in the closing lines of Goethe's *Faust*. 'The feminine is that element in the world which strives outward in order to be fructified by the eternal element of life.'[15]

Spica Virginis (*Spica*—Latin for ear of grain) in the Virgo constellation is the fifteenth brightest star in the sky. It is more or less the same brightness as Antares in the constellation of Scorpio. Spica is a binary star, each one much larger than our sun.

Virgo is part of a section of the Milky Way called, in ancient China, The Dragon of the East. This is one of the four dragons of the Milky Way and its ideogram JIAO XIU means a wise majestic incarnation of the awesome power and infinite splendour of nature presiding over the metamorphosis of the whole of creation.[16] Spica is the eye of this dragon. That is why Lilith became known also as a great seductress, luring mankind into the beauty and pleasure of nature, with the risk of leading us into animal consciousness and separating us from our spiritual origin and journey. This danger was real due to man's power to handle the elemental spirits which accompany the four states of matter.

In the last 150 years scientists identified 92 natural elements (periodic table) and grouped them in an ingenious way into a table of reactivity. All of them have three states according to the amount of heat in them. Modern science doesn't consider heat a state of matter, but calls this huge area of the electromagnetic spectrum infrared.

The ancient Greek civilization perceived the material world made of four elements, each with an etheric intelligent function.

The Greek earth element means that the solid state is coupled with the life ether. This life ether allows forms to arise from inside out from a seed, egg and bud according to the kind of spirit incarnating in the genetic plan that produces substances. Life ether rejuvenates, creates inner mobility and realizes a totality in a context of equilibrium (health) whereas the solid state is fixed, crystal-like, impenetrable, allowing a stable external form.[17] Understanding the landscape of the lung in depth helps us to grasp the life ether.

The water element means the liquid state is accompanied by the chemical or sound ether. The liquid state forms drops that fuse together when they touch and flow, influenced by gravity (think of liquid mercury or dew). The chemical/sound ether forms intervals (music doesn't exist without it) and is also discrete (composed of separate parts). Substances behave chemically according to the law of numbers. Like music, the whole periodic table can be arranged in octaves on a scale of increasing atomic weight and reactivity.[17]

The periodic table has in fact been studied on the octave scale by the American natural philosopher Walter Russell in his book *The Universal One.* Understanding the landscape of the liver in depth helps us to grasp the chemical/sound/music/number ether.

The air element means the gaseous state coupled with the light ether. The gas fills the space and links together the objects, whereas the light ether separates the objects by lighting their surfaces. The former is unstructured, elastic, compressible, tending to expand into space, exercises a pressure and penetrates biological membranes. The light ether, on the other hand, is structured and breakable, radiating in straight lines, and makes space visible. Our eyes perceive the electromagnetic frequencies of light but not the subtle influences it carries from the sun.[17] Understanding the landscape of the kidney in depth helps us to grasp the light ether inside us.

The fire element means the heat state with its warmth ether. The fire element, when too intense, makes the objects disappear from the world of perception, whereas warmth is an intensive movement penetrating everything and allowing metamorphoses. The warmth ether leads the way towards the world of living phenomena through the birth and ripening process.

Heat state is a time that dissipates and destroys, and warm-blooded animals spend a lot of energy maintaining the fulcrum point (c. 37 degrees centigrade). The warmth ether is a creative time that carries subtle influences sucked in by the sun from the stars.[17] Warmth ether is everywhere in us. It dwells mostly in the heart-blood flow and our spirit lives in the warmth of that pulsing flow.

The first three states/ethers are seen as densified heat state/warmth ether. In the same way, the modern models in astronomy usually start with a very hot beginning for the universe (the

Big Bang model is just one). In the intense heat on the surface of the sun only hydrogen and helium can form. A million times bigger than the earth, the sun, at its centre, is infinitely hot. Like the appearance of the first cell, the formation of atoms in these immemorial times is far from being understood.

We owe to Steiner and his followers the development of the relation between the four states of matter and the etheric forces coupled with them. The workings of the four pairs above are not the same as the formative forces coming from the stars. These pairs are like the builders of all trades when a house is in construction, following the blueprint of the architect. Because these four ethers border the physical we have the capacity sometimes to perceive them (elemental beings). We perceive light but do we really capture the essence of this mysterious phenomenon? No, and that's why science is still studying light—it hasn't yet revealed all its secrets. So it is for the other ethers. In *Occult Science* Steiner described the progressive appearance of these four couples in the course of the evolution of the solar system, starting with the heat state/warmth ether.

These four ethers spread to the stars like an invisible sea of intelligent activity. The entities of the twelve star system stimulate the beings of the four ethers and generate the formative forces. Steiner called this association (formative forces and the four ethers) the cosmic Verb. Matter emerges out of this association where formative forces become forms. The four kingdoms are material forms. This is a descending movement from the spirit world to materiality. Having achieved that, there is another movement, ascending this time, from organic or inorganic matter to processes. Steiner preferred the expression 'unfolding rhythm'[17] instead of process.

Each material substance, living or inert, is an unique architectural construction (a molecular signature) that emits a kind of 'resonance' or 'oscillation' that can be used to heal. The resonance of this process or activity can be transferred into water by dilution/succussion. Our body, too, by constantly diluting metallic enzymatic co-factors is in this polarity. It is well known in physics and biology that when matter is highly diluted (near atomic level or beyond when only the oscillation is preserved) it manifests more its own activity side. A very small amount of arsenic or germanium makes silicon a semiconductor.

On the other hand, with curative eurythmy or Hauschka massage, we move in the polarity of formative forces/forms (descending activity). So it is with preparation 501 in biodynamic farming where silica powder in a horn (antenna) will capture in the course of the summer the sun forces. It is the water on the surface of the silica crystals that holds the summer sun influences.

'These four principles, formative force, form, matter and process are never isolated in nature.'[17] The blueprint of an architect for the construction of a house is living in the mind of the builders of all trades. It is not energy or matter. The formative forces can be compared simplistically to the blueprint. But the architect first obeys the intention of a spirit. Each species has an intentional spirit that activates the production of its own architecture.

The activity of states of matter and their ethers generates a shadow or sub-ether. We know that when we rarefy a gas in a glass tube and send an electric current into it, then we produce light – the fluorescent bulb or neon. In our energy-saving light bulbs we might have mercury gases. In our yellow street lamps we might have a sodium gas. The gas state of matter and its light ether are an active couple that links with a sub-ether called electricity. We haven't yet found the relation between the liquid state with its sound/chemical ether that links with the magnetic force. Steiner talked about a 'third force' generated by the solid state with its life ether. These sub-forces exist because of the emergence of the material world.

Due to our exclusive focus on the sensible world and its sub-earthly forces, science and its technological arm have produced the world we live in now. In the future, mankind will turn his gaze towards the ever-present super-sensible forces.

Applied material properties in technology are not good or bad, but it does change our relation with the natural world. It is our use of it that makes it destructive or constructive.

It will be the task of the good, healing science to find certain cosmic forces which can reach the earth through the co-operation of two cosmic streams, those of Pisces and Virgo. The great secret to be discovered will be how the influence which works from the direction of Pisces as a power of the sun unites itself with the influence working from the direction of Virgo.... When the forces of Pisces and Virgo act in co-operation, nothing wrongful can be brought into being. Men will achieve something through which the mechanism of life will be detached, in a certain sense, from man himself, but will not give any one group power and rulership over another. The cosmic forces drawn from this direction will create remarkable machines, but only those that will relieve man of work, because they will carry a certain power of intelligence within themselves.[18]

Virgo as sodium (Na) is part of the hydrosphere cross with Pisces as chorine (Cl).The properties of these two elements are polar opposites, yet complementary. So it is for Gemini as sulphur (S) and Sagittarius as magnesium (Mg). Na/Cl (sodium chloride or table salt) or Mg/S (Magnesium sulphate) form the basic salts of the ocean, as well as the background of all organic liquids pulsing through living species.[19]

Hydrosphere or the basic salts of the sea (salt cross — sodium chloride and magnesium sulphate)

Virgo (sodium)

Gemini (sulphur)   Sagittarius (magnesium)

Pisces (chorine)

If we assemble the twelve major elements treated in this study, so essential for life, we realize that they form the material basis of the biosphere (Fig. 1). The cross above forms the hydrosphere (basic salts of the ocean). Another cross holds the elements that form the atmosphere — the basis of the organic world (see the end of the Scorpio text). The third is the mineral cross and forms the basic elements of the solid crust: geosphere (see the end of the Libra text).

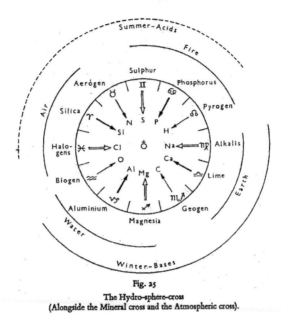

Fig. 25
The Hydro-sphere-cross
(Alongside the Mineral cross and the Atmospheric cross).

Fig. 1 *The zodiac circle of the elements with its three crosses by R. Hauschka in* The Nature of Substance

12. Leo

Preamble

The word energy comes from the Greek *energeia* (*en*: within, *ergon*: work): a work in action or a power to modify the state of other systems with which it interacts.

Energy, however, is not simply heat or electric power but can take many forms. The smell of an onion can induce tears in the eye, and because of that it can be seen as energy. Aroma is the most evanescent of creation. Transforming food (baking bread) also produces aroma. We live constantly in an ocean of flavours. In essence these subtle emanations are gaseous. And, like all gases, they expand in space applying pressure on solid objects, easily penetrating water and biological membranes and impacting our internal environment. When we enter a restaurant the aroma pervading the air has a direct influence on our digestion and we start to salivate and secrete juices in the stomach. The more hydrogen (Leo) in a substance the more gaseous and flammable it is, like essential oil.

All sensory impressions are energy but are not always considered as such in science. There is a need to widen the concept of energy in physics but this is difficult because:

> ... a physics arose (mid nineteenth century) that sees the salvation of physics in considering physical facts separately from the human being. This is indeed the principal characteristic of modern physics. Many publications proclaim this idea as necessary for the advancement of physics, stating that nothing must be introduced that comes from the human being himself ... that has to do with his own organic processes. But in this way we shall arrive at nothing.[1]

Traditional Chinese medicine calls aroma a kind of chi (energy force) because it impacts on the activity of organs and creates ideograms as images of these activities. The ideograms stand for an inner process rather than a concept or object in space. To grasp an ideogram we need to set in motion an image of the process in our feeling life. To 'set in motion' is the essence of chi.

'Life processes are in constant movement and cannot be grasped with the closed mind suitable for calculation; you require concepts mobile in themselves—pictures. The etheric man within the fluid man is apprehended in pictures.'[2]

Because chi is an activity it is also a kind of will.

'Everything in the world of senses is will, a strong and powerful current of will.... The world of the senses thus becomes, as it were, a sea of infinitely differentiated will.'[3]

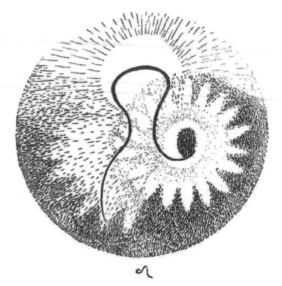

The Constellation of Leo (Lion)

Content

This text explores the imprint of the intelligent activity of Leo all around us in the constant forming of human and animal creation. What is the relation between the Leo sector of space, its glyph, the medieval image of this constellation, Imma's drawing, the element hydrogen, the animal phylum mammal, the life sense, the heart pulsation, sun as a ruling sphere, the colour yellow and the consonants T and D? Based on Imma's drawings in the first edition of *The Calendar of the Soul* in 1912, we can try to find a golden thread linking the various ways Leo acts as a constant blueprint in nature.

Description of the Glyph and Traditional Image

This glyph reminds us of a single agitated whiplash. In this gesture something shows an individualized circulatory process.

The traditional picture shows an alert standing lion ready for action. A lion lives largely in its heart/lung rhythmic complex and is revered as the king of the animals. Its well developed muscular system gives it great elasticity of tissues, speed, agility and autonomy.

Description of the Drawing

The top of the drawing is dominated by a huge sun that seems to be rising behind a hill. It looks like a new dawn.

On the right we see a dark egg shape in the middle of a clear round halo irradiating *18* petals, a number expressing 'life in its fullness'.[4] These petals are rays parting the surrounding dark. Inside the flower at the bottom of the dark oval we have the start of a long expressive dark wavy line moving up into the sun before moving down towards the bottom darker left periphery. The thickness of this line decreases progressively as it reaches the bottom.

Towards the left side we notice *seven* further rays of light: 'the number of time'.[5] These are behind the whiplash and emanate from the 18-petalled flower. This central whiplash is like the traditional Leo sign and reminds us of a flagellated Protozoa or a spermatozoid. It fills the drawing with a circulatory organizing pulse. Its flagellum starts in the flower, goes to the sun first before descending to the dense earth.There is primal linking activity here.

Hydrogen: The First Element

Through the progressive cooling of the expanding physical universe, the first element appeared: hydrogen—Leo in matter. Helium is the second simplest element and forms, with hydrogen, 99 per cent of the material universe. Hydrogen is the baby element, the first to appear in this extreme heat from which the others will follow. Hydrogen lifts in the air, seemingly unaffected by gravity. At ground level it is 2 per cent of the air, whereas at 100 km up it forms 99 per cent of a very hot layer surrounding the earth (the thermosphere). When hydrogen is the predominant atom, organic substances tend to be in their gaseous state, expanding into the air escaping gravity (methane (CH_4) or all essential oils).

Hydrogen in the organic world is a dematerializing element bringing the essence of things upwards. The word hydrogen means water generator when linked with oxygen, but when it is alone it is explosive. It is the hottest flame. After all it is the closest element to the heat state of matter. In all the kingdoms its ionic form (H+) determines the level of acidity (pH). In our bodies we spend a lot of energy to maintain the right level of acidity. Hydrogen is so reactive that it can dissolve metals.

In the drawing the whiplash form is standing alone, suggesting hydrogen's primal nature. We find it in abundance on the surface of the sun where the temperature is cooling down from the infinite heat of the centre.

Mammals: The Furry Warm-Blooded Ones

Mammal: c. 4,400 species
With Leo we enter into the last phylum: the mammals. Already alive during the great Saurian expansion, the early emerging

mammals couldn't develop fully because of the ferocity of the reptiles and were living underground or in the undergrowth of primeval forests.

One of these was the solenodon. It is a shrew-like animal the size of a rabbit and still alive today and found in the Caribbean islands.

Then great geological and atmospheric changes brought more cold, detrimental to the cold-blooded reptiles, allowing the warm-blooded mammals to express their full potential.

Mammals took major steps by controlling their internal heat with layers of fat, fur and complex homeostatic controls. With a uterus they have fewer babies but in this warm space gestation is safer. Warm milk and the protection of the parents ensure a better survival of the newborn. We also observe for the first time a separation between the thoracic cavity and the abdomen with the main breathing muscle: the diaphragm.

As we saw with the birds (Virgo), different species in this phylum also explore their place in the inherent threefoldness of nature. In some the metabolic process predominates (cow). In others the rhythmic system is more apparent (lion). As for the head centre, it is more developed in the primates and marine mammals (dolphin).

The more this phylum develops the more the three organic centres: head, thorax and abdomen become more complex. This organic complexity goes hand-in-hand with greater consciousness and more refined instinctual behaviours.

Sense of Life: Inner Environment Reaches Our Consciousness

From inside our organism all sorts of messages come to our consciousness. They help us feel the life inside us in manifold ways. I am in pain, I am tired, I am hungry, I feel sick, I feel refreshed … The list is long and these messages are not always easy to decipher. For instance, a burning sensation at the bottom of the shoulder blade might indicate problems in the gall bladder (referred pain). Our sense of life registers this.

All animals have a nervous system and a subtle sense of life. As they evolve, more complex brain hemispheres give them a greater consciousness of their own sense of life and the ability to respond to what is happening inside them.

A Circulatory Individualized Warm Flow

The spirit in incarnation needs a degree of warmth that comes from the environment for most living creatures. Birds and mammals are equipped to maintain their internal warmth. When the cold season comes they develop strategies. If birds or mammals can find enough food they endure a winter even at minus 40 degrees. Others migrate where they can find food or hibernate with enough reserve fat to maintain the vital organs at the right temperature through the winter.

Warm blood circulation comes very early in the embryo of mammals and synchronizes with the mother's even before the appearance of the heart. The whiplash in Imma's drawing represents the essence of a warm circulatory pulse essential in all mammals.

Warm-blooded animals have a psychic life made of urges, desires. It is there that the actual impulse of blood movement is found.

'It is the feeling of the soul which gives rise to the movement of the blood.'[6]

The Sun Sphere Rules Leo

We live inside the flow of nature's rhythms and our life depends on the rhythmic flow of the blood/heart stream. The blood is the only tissue that flows into the intimacy of each organ to bring substances and subtle influences. In turn, each organ transforms the blood stream in its own unique way.

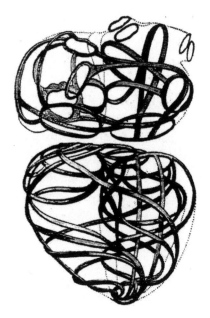

Fig. 1 *The movement of water spiralling around a vortex.* Sensitive Chaos *by Theodor Schwenk*

Fig. 2 *The tendons of the heart. Part of this picture (left ventricle) is shown in* Sensitive Chaos, *and comes from a German book by Benninghoff, 1925*

The sun's 'rhythmic enfoldment' has to do with circulation.

'According to [Steiner] it is not the heart that moves the blood, but the blood that moves the heart.'[7]

The tendons of the heart (Fig. 1) are very similar to the movement of water around a vortex (Fig. 2). This is not surprising when we realize that nowhere else in the body is the blood shaken so strongly. The vigorous contractions of the heart generate thousands of vortices. This primal vortex form is seen everywhere, in star systems as well as in air (twister) and water (whirlpool) movements.

Subtle influences can come from the stars as formative forces (super-sensible world), from nature's kingdoms as processes (sensible world) or from the sub-sensible realm as pulsed electricity and magnetism. Water or blood in motion is open to all these influences.

When water is shaken, vortices can pick up the oscillation or vibratory frequency and imprint them into the water. All living molecular architectures or inorganic substances have a fingerprint or resonance of some sort. A water vortex is an ear/transducer/pencil bringing subtle influences into the water's micro-structure. In all cases water can hold the memory of these 'oscillations' or 'rhythmic unfoldments'[8] for a while when diluted and succussed (shaken) properly.

Our organs all the time dilute blood substances to the right ratio (the kidneys do this thousands of times a day) and the heart, by its succussing activity, transfers the oscillating aspect into the blood flow. It's not only food and waste that circulate in our blood. Multiple subtle influences travel in the blood.

Even what comes from our sense organs as impressions are captured and preserved by the brain. To reach our consciousness as pictures, specific breathing pulses (Mars process) need to be present around the grey matter. The blood flow captures these pictorial impressions and distributes them as formative impulses or morphic fields everywhere in the body. Sense impressions are pictorial for our consciousness and formative for our internal organs.

'These images [morphic fields] that we breathe in [through our senses] are diffused in the whole body by the life of the circulation (sun). This life of the circulation is in connection with the metabolism (Mercury process) and it is there that the substances start to integrate itself to the images [or morphic fields].'[9]

We can see that the percepts don't feed only our inner psychic landscape but are form-fields for our physical landscape. With the sun process the circulatory system brings these images/ blueprints as morphic fields of organs to the whole body.

Leo is inseparable from its ruler, the sun. The sun, through its heat, promotes circulation in air/oceanic currents. In us, the heart regulates the blood flow. The sun with Leo provides the physical landscape (heart/blood circulation) that supplies the body's specific rhythms.

The ancient Egyptians knew the heart as a dwelling place for their spirit. Except for skin, bones and muscle, the heart was the only internal organ they mummified.

'We must know that, in spite of the fact that they are not fully impregnated with conscious life, all the organs contain the source of the surge directing us towards the psychic life.'[10]

The psychic entity of the heart or its creative spirit is called *shen* in ancient Chinese physiology.[11] Its function relates with the global intuitive intelligence that allows inner perception coming from a realm beyond the physical. Psychologists and scientists call it insight. It is a sudden illumination in regard to their work, but do they really understand where it comes from? They usually sidestep the question by saying it is the mark of a genius.

When we are asleep there is no tone in our muscles. The fact of being conscious brings a minimum of tonality (constant nervous influx) in our skeletal muscles even if we are totally relaxed. But the sensation that enters the sense organ needs to meet an intention to see it. Our eyes might be open but if we are too busy inside our own mind we don't see anything consciously. To operate properly the sense organs and their nerves need the intention of a spirit. The sense nerves are also motor nerves and vice versa. It is a two way stream of activity.

As British physicist James Dyson (1914–1990) said 'Don't think that your will is synonymous with your intention … Motor nerves are sensory to the intention [of the spirit in incarnation].'[12]

Consonants T and D

To make the sound T or D we need to build up an air pressure by contracting the abdominal muscles, while the tip of the tongue blocks the air behind the gum ridge of the upper teeth. When the tongue releases its pressure in a whiplash movement, these consonants can be uttered. There is a kind of pressure-relaxation operating here, a bit like the systole-diastole rhythm of the heart. These sounds awaken the tongue. In Chinese energetics, the tongue is seen as the bud of the heart.

'T is the sound that wants to penetrate in from the top of our heads to the ends of our toes (the eurythmy gesture for T is suggesting that). It wants to help us complete the process of entering into our physical body … this is the sound … of spirit penetrating into matter.'[13]

Conclusion

One of the main stars in this constellation is the exceedingly
bright Regulus star which in ancient myth is called the Ruler or
Lawgiver.[14]

Leo is the prompter of matter's mobility. It is an organizing
linking force with a goal. This goal is to allow a flow that links a
centre of command (a spirit) with a construction site (the body
structure). Things need to be in a moving flow in order for a form
to appear.

In Imma's drawing life in its fullness (the number 18)
expresses itself through a time process (the number seven) in the
material world by uniting the subtle influences that the sun
brings within matter. In the drawing the flagellum starts in the
18-petalled flower emanating seven rays and moves upwards to
the sun before going down into matter — bringing the heat and
light charged with the subtle formative influences of the stars.
This flowing link is essential for the expression of all living
creatures.

'If in old age one has an interest that completely occupies one's
soul and spirit, something that inspires and enthuses one, this
makes one youthful. The meaning of "inspiration" is that
something spiritual enters the mind.... Being filled with
enthusiasm is indeed a source of rejuvenation.'[15]

Leo's intelligent activity is like an enthused foreman on the
construction site. He is the one who obeys the original intention
with the images provided by the architect and organizes the
builders of all trades for the emergence of a house, in order for
the form to appear in space. In each of our cells the foreman is the
ribosomes. According to where the cell is, the centre of command
(the nucleolus of the nucleus) orders the production of specific
proteins. The order is carried out in the cytoplasm by the ribosomes that organize the production of substances. Ribosomes are
also responsible for the creation of a complex matrix of fibres in
the cytoplasm linking all the organelles together.

In a previous chapter we mentioned Steiner's suggestion that the sun is a kind of three dimensional dark hole in a fabric of the space-time continuum, sucking the subtle influences of the constellation behind through to the earth. It seems that the realm of beyond space and time (counterspace) where these spiritual forces come from is infinitely hot and charged with a meta-morphic potential. Light on its own is not enough for plant growth; we need a daily sunrise or a seasonal spring to coax life into expression with the right amount of heat.

Afterword

One of the enduring mysteries of biology in the twenty-first century is form. How are biological forms created and sustained? Why are insects and buds and fingers and trees and humans the shape that they are? How do cells know how to grow into certain shapes according to where they are in an organism? The embryologist Rupert Sheldrake stipulated that a kind of phantom energy field exists that defines the shapes of living beings in his Morphogenic Field theory. Even this is only a partial solution. How is the field generated and what influences it?

These are ideas that we have explored. To find answers we have had to move beyond conventional science. Modern science has developed into a too-rigid framework of measurable evidence and 'objective' observation. The history of the development of science is perhaps a tale for another book but it often seems that as a knee-jerk reaction to finally separate from the Church and spirituality, science has been too quick to dismiss methods and avenues of enquiry that are as equally valid as the current scientific method. Methods that are more subjective or even spiritual are seen as unscientific and therefore necessarily invalid and to be ignored.

We have followed the zodiac in an anticlockwise movement revealing the progressive ascent of the animal phyla expression towards self-consciousness. This is the story of evolution on earth but not as it is usually told. This is not purely evolution by natural selection and chance mutations. Evolution here is purposeful with intelligence activities.

From a highly sensitive membrane enclosure that can pulse to a thorax, *Cancer* creates a semi-closed centre where pulsating spirits can dwell. It is not a heart or lung yet, but a porous container for them. From there the spirited centre has the impulse to extend in space, to move and grasp the world. From tentacles to shoulders and arms, *Gemini* generates, in this budding, a lateral bisymmetry to grasp the world. Out of this centre a spirit urge is there to listen to the vibrations of the world. From the listening of mouth-hand/finger creatures (starfish) to the neck/larynx/ear in mammals, *Taurus* invites an instrument that can hear which is the first step before the power to speak (larynx). And last, from a notochord in tunicata to our own central nervous system, *Aries* offers progressively a round cranium to shelter a reflector of thought forms (the brain) for the spirit in incarnation. In this succession we have an upwards movement, considering our verticality. The progressive appearances of these phyla had and still have an important role in the construction of earth's bio-sphere.

From the various slimy poda to the feet, *Pisces* brings the instrument that grounds us to firm earth — a dense ground for a destiny to walk upon. From these myriads of moving muscular cylinders (worms) comes a way to move substances in us (vascular and digestive systems). *Aquarius* offers great flowing possibilities for the feet (dancing) that listen and act in the world. From an external articulated skeleton (arthropoda) to an internal articulated bone structure, *Capricorn* invents ways to join and articulate various moving parts to increase flexibility and mobility. *Sagittarius* goes from fish to thigh — two propulsors shooting in one direction. We have with these four creations another upward direction from feet to thigh.

Scorpio orients us toward meiotic division (sexual differentiation). Not only our fingerprints but on the membrane of each of our cells there is a marker of our own individuality. *Libra* looks for a point of balance between the heavy head, thorax, abdomen and legs. The hips can transfer the load to two legs but a fulcrum point is needed at the junction sacrum/hip. Fulcrum points are numerous at all levels of our existence. Existence is a knife-edge venture at all levels. *Virgo* rules the nourishing belly (milky intestinal chyme) with its capacity to invite a new incarnation (uterus). Then comes *Leo*, the pulsation activity that connects the celestial formative with the terrestrial density insuring a constant flow. From the sexual organs to a permanent pulsing flow of liquids in us we have our third upward movement.

If our physical threefoldness expresses itself in an vertically-upwards architecture, is it possible that this expression reverberates in our psychic life with a longing to go upwards in our psychic development by mastering our animality?

All the instinctive behaviour of animals we have in us. By mastering these reactive animal forces man's spirit has more chance to be in touch with his destiny.

All the active intelligence of the plant construction we have in us *too*. That is why it can heal various dysfunctions of our organs. It is often asked if plants have a soul. *Conscious* soul activity starts with the animals because they link perceptual organs with a muscular movement through a network of nerves (brain). Nevertheless plants have a great sensitivity: heliotropism of what is above the ground and geotropism that leads the roots towards the dark fertile ground. More intriguing is the fact that they transform in some plant species proteins into alkaloids (nicotine, caffeine, cocaine, opium and other hallucinogenic substances). All this has a direct impact on *our psyche*, the way we think, feel and will the world. This indicates that the Beings of plants do have a soul around them without its instrument of incarnation (*neuronal connections*) and in some *plant species* allows the formation of alkaloids.

As we have seen, these influences from the constellations each act in turn to foster specific evolutionary phases throughout the history of life on earth. Just as importantly, however, is the fact that these forces are continuously influencing all biological entities and it is in humans that they currently culminate. These influences from the constellations are the underlying blueprint which informs our form. *They rebuild us all the time.*

The constellations of the zodiac exert the most subtle of influences and are undetected and even unacknowledged by modern science and yet they underpin our very existence — *how we are* here *physically* for a while *in the realm of density.*

Notes

Introduction

1. R. Steiner to Edith Maryon 26 Dec. 1922, GA 40.
2. *The Theosophy of Friedrich Christoph Oetinger* by Carl August Auberlen, 1847.
3. Comment by Steiner on *The Theosophy of Friedrich Christoph Oetinger* by Carl August Auberlen, 1847.
4. Audrey E. McAllen in *The Listening Ear*, Hawthorn Press, 1989. A facsimile of the first *Calendar of the Soul* by Christopher Bamford can be found at Steiner House Library.
5. Rudolf Steiner's *Calendar of the Soul*, by Margot Rossler, Anthroposophical Quarterly, Vol. 3, No. 1, spring 1958.
6. R. Steiner in *Initiation, Eternity and the Passing Moment*, Lecture 1, Munich, 25 Aug., 1912.
7. J.A. Wheeler *In Mehra*.
8. This information re. the elements and the constellations was explored by R. Hauschka in *The Nature of Substance*.
9. Eugen Kolisko in his booklets *Zoology for Everybody*.
10. Several lectures by Steiner may be consulted: 'Man's Twelve Senses in their Relation to Imagination, Inspiration and Intuition', Dornach, 8 August, 1920; 'Le Zodiac et les 12 Sens', Dornach, 12 and 13 August, 1916; 'Man as a Being of Sense Perception', July 22, 23, 24, 1921. Steiner's drawings of the twelve senses and the constellations in his Notebooks present another point of view studied by Albert Soesman in *The Twelve Senses*, Hawthorn Press. It is an honest attempt to grasp this complex image but is not mentioned here because there is no text accompanying it.
11. A. McAllen in *The Listening Ear*. Imma von Eckardstein's drawings are in this book, as are the twelfth century pictures of the zodiac from the Hunterian Psalter (M. S. Hunter 229), Glasgow University Library. Imma von Eckardstein's drawings can also be found in the facsimile of *The Calendar of the Soul* first produced in 1912, in an edition edited by C. Bamford, SteinerBooks, 2003.

12. Steiner in 'Discussion with the Goetheanum workmen', 2 August, 1922 on the origin of speech and language.
13. Goethe in *The Theory of Colours*.
14. Steiner in *The Arts and their Mission*, Anthroposophic Press, 1964.
15. Steiner in 'The Human Being and the Forms of Eurythmy', Dornach, 7 July, 1924.
16. Steiner in 'Cours d' Eurythmy de la Parole', GA 279.
17. Steiner in *Anthroposophy And The Inner Life*. Nine lectures, Dornach, 19 Jan. to 10 Feb. 1924.

Chapter 1

1. In *The Lord's Prayer and Rudolf Steiner* by Peter Selg, Floris Books.
2. R. Steiner in *Theosophy*, chap. 3.
3. R. Steiner in 'Centre of Ancient Mysteries', fifth lecture, 1923. Details of that were given also in Berlin, 9 February, 1911 in 'Was hat die Geologie uber Weltentstehung zu sagen'.
4. R. Steiner, from the Aphorisms on the elements in his Notebook, 1924 cited by W. Pelikan in his book *Man and the Medicinal Plants* Tome 3, (Valerian chapter). These aphorisms were given to him by Guenther Wachsmuth.
5. AMP, ADP and ATP stand for adenosine mono, di and triphosphate. Phosphate is one of the organic forms of phosphorus in us. It is a very important component of each cell and forms highly energetic compounds like AMP for hormonal activities inside the cell. Also when the glucose is burnt in the mitochondria of cells with the help of oxygen, ATP–ADP become essential to hold and carry this energy where it is needed. At a molecular level in this tiny drop of gelatinous liquid we can assume that these transfers of energy verge close to the speed of light.
6. James Lovelock in *Gaia* discussing Margulis' hypothesis of endosymbiosis. Bacteria, as the first living organisms, incorporated themselves into the bigger unicellular cells. They became mitochondria in animal cells or chloroplasts in plant cells. They have similar sizes and the same function: they handle energy. They carry their own genetic material allowing them to reproduce according to the need of the bigger host cells.

Bacteria: because their genetic material is free in the cytoplasm and not contained inside a nucleus, bacteria can easily exchange genetic matter. This is why some microbiologists considered bacteria as one species acting like the digestive system of the planet. (Sorin Sonea and Maurice Panisset in *Introduction a la nouvelle bacteriologie*, Presses de l'Université de Montréal, Masson, 1980.)

7. Margulis & Sagan in *The Micro-Cosmos*.
8. Werner Schupbach in *New Perspectives in Biology*.
9. Eugen Kolisko, *Zoology for Everybody*, No. 4.
10. Some confusion exists concerning the twelve senses and their relation to specific constellations. Steiner gave several lectures concerning this. The main lectures used here are 'Forming of Man through Cosmic Influences', Dornach, 8 Oct.–5 Nov, 1921 and 'Man's Twelve Senses in Their Relation to Imagination, Inspiration, Intuition', Dornach, 8 August 1920. Nevertheless, another drawing (of the senses and constellations) was found in Steiner's Notebook without a text and Albert Soesman in his book *Our Twelve Senses* makes an interesting attempt to decipher it.
11. Entelechy is from Greek *en*: within, *telos*: perfection, *ekhein*: maintain a certain state by continuing effort—meaning to be in a certain state of perfection within. Aristotle developed this word in his philosophy to try to explain a vital force or energy directing life expression, its movement, its growth and the maintenance of intricate forms.
12. A. McAllen in *The Listening Ear*.
13. Brunhild Müller in *Painting with Children*, Floris Books, 2010.
14. Goethe in *The Theory of Colours*.
15. David Whyte in *Consolation*, Many Rivers Press, 2015.
16. R. Steiner in *The Being of Man and his Future Evolution*, Lecture 8, 3 May, 1909.

Chapter 2

1. R. Steiner quoted by Dr Rita Leroy in *Illness and Healing*.
2. R. Steiner, in *Occult Physiology*.
3. Ibid.
4. Alexis Carrel in *Man, The Unknown*.

5. R. Steiner in *Occult Physiology*.
6. Ibid.
7. R. Hauschka in *The Nature of Substance*.
8. Steiner in his Notebooks from W. Pelikan in *Man and the Medicinal Plants*, Tome 3 in the chapter on the Valerianaceae. This information was given to Pelikan by Guenther Wachsmuth.
9. Wilhelm Pelikan in *The Secrets of Metals*.
10. Inspired by *The Nature of Substance* by R. Hauschka.
11. Wilhelm Pelikan quoting R. Steiner in *L'Homme et les Plantes Médicinales*.
12. *A New Zoology* by H. Poppelbaum.
13. Ibid.
14. *The Fifth Miracle* by Paul Davies.
15. *La Science Comme Mythe* by Y. Johannisse, G. Lane.
16. Steiner in Notebooks. (See Note 8.)
17. Dr Rita Leroi quoting R. Steiner in her *Illness and Healing*.
18. Steiner in 'Forming of Man through Cosmic Influences', Dornach, 28 October, 1921.
19. From *The Seven Metabolic Processes* by Dr Ross Rentea.
20. Steiner in 'The Planets and their Life Qualities', Dornach, 29 Oct. 1921.
21. A. McAllen in *The Listening Ear*.
22. *Zoology for Everybody* No. 5, Eugen Kolisko.

Chapter 3

1. Lebanese-American poet Kahlil Gibran (1883–1931) in the poem *On my birthday*, 1910. Strongly influenced by his discovery of William Blake, Gibran wrote, he had 'come upon a soul who is a sister to my soul', *Kahlil Gibran, Man and Poet* by Suheil Bushrui and Joe Jenkins.
2. Callahan, Philip, *Exploring the Spectrum*, 1984 and *Tuning into Nature*, Acres, 1974.
3. R. Hauschka in *The Nature of Substance*.
4. Ibid.
5. R. Steiner (see chap. 1, Note 4).
6. R. Steiner, in 'Forming of Man through Cosmic Influences', Dornach, 28 October–5 November, 1921.

7. R. Steiner in 'Principles of Psychosomatic Physiology', chap. 7.
8. H. Poppelbaum in *A New Zoology*.
9. A. McAllen, *The Listening Ear*.
10. Recommended reading: John Martineau in *A Little Book of Coincidence in the Solar System*, Wooden Books Ltd, 2012. And also Joachim Schultz in *Movements and Rhythms of the Stars*, Floris Books.

Chapter 4

1. Steiner in 'Douze Harmony Zodiacal', 18 December 1920 (about the alphabet).
2. In physics today scientists work with five forces in relation to matter: gravity, electricity, magnetism and two more in connection with the atom structure: the weak and the strong force.
3. W. Sucker in *Lecture to Experimental Circle*, Peredur, 1956.
4. Steiner in 'Forming of Man through Cosmic Influences', Dornach, 1921.
5. Robert Sardello in *Power of Soul (Living The Twelve Virtues)*.
6. Steiner in his Notebooks. (See Note 4 in chapter one.)
7. The information on silica comes from *The Nature of Substance* by R. Hauschka.
8. Robert Sardello in *The Power of Soul*.
9. W. Sucker (see Note 3).
10. Hartmut Warm in *The Signature of the Celestial Spheres*.
11. The *Physiology Coloring Book* by W. Kapit, R. I. Macey and E. Meisami.
12. Steiner in 'Forming of Man', Dornach 29 Oct. 1921.
13. A. McAllen in *The Listening Ear*.
14. E. Kolisko in *Zoology for Everybody*.

Chapter 5

1. Steiner in *Man's Being, His destiny and World Evolution* (GA 226).
2. Steiner in *The World of the Senses and the World of the Spirit*, Lecture I and 2.
3. Robert Sardello in *The Power of Soul*.

4. David Bohm in *Wholeness and the Implicate Order*, 1980.
5. Robert Sardello in *The Power of Soul*, Hampton Roads, 2002.
6. Audrey McAllen in *The Listening Ear*.
7. James Lovelock in *Gaia*, Gaia Books, 1991.
8. Eugen Kolisko in *Zoology for Everybody*, No. 6, Kolisko Archive Publication, 1981.
9. A. Besant and C. W. Leadbeater in *Occult Chemistry*. The ANU was described by these authors as the ultimate particle—in fact there are two, one turning clockwise and the other anticlockwise. They are lovely beating heart-shaped vortices. Besant and Leadbeater cultivated a yogic technique that allowed their conscious mind to descend into the infinitely small atom and slow down the construction to see the architecture of elements known at that time (c. 1900). The investigation predicted some new elements not known at that time. Steiner never contested their theosophical findings but did scold them for working only in a materialistic way at the ultimate fragmentation of matter. He said that there were questions they should have asked: where do these strange constructions come from? What are the formative entities behind them? Then they would have had to turn their gaze towards the pulsing star systems and consider the progressive evolution of the earth.
10. Jacques Benveniste is a French immunologist who made controversial experiments on high dilution around 1985. He showed that the oscillation pattern of a molecule can leave an active trace in the water micro-structure if well succussed after dilution.
11. Kolisko in *Zoology for Everybody*.
12. Annick de Souzenelle in *Le symbolisme du corps humain*, 1984.
13. A. McAllen in *The Listening Ear*.
14. Steiner, GA 208, Dornach, 28 Oct. 1921.

Chapter 6

1. Steiner in discussions with the workmen, 18 Sept. 1924, in *From Beetroot to Buddism*, Rudolf Steiner Press, 1999.
2. W. Sucher in *Lectures to Experimental Circle at Peredur*, Lect. 2, 10 Jan. 1956.

3. Steiner in *The Mystery of the Universe*, Lect. 15, 15 May, 1920.
4. Steiner in his Notebooks 1924. See Note 4 in chapter 1 (Cancer).
5. Rudolf Hauschka in *The Nature of Substance*, Vincent Stuart and John M. Watkins Ltd., 1966.
6. W. Sucher, see Note 2.
7. A. E. McAllen in *The Listening Ear*.
8. Gary Goldschneider and Joost Elffers in *The Secret Language of Birthdays*, Element Books Ltd, 1998.
9. Same as Note 7.

Chapter 7

1. R. Hauschka in *The Nature of Substance*.
2. H. Poppelbaum in *A New Zoology*, chap. 17.
3. A. McAllen in *The Listening Ear*.
4. Steiner, 29 Oct. 1921, Dornach, RLXXVI – Vol. 1.
5. Steiner in *Occult Physiology*.
6. Steiner, quoted by A. McAllen in *The Listening ear*.
7. A. McAllen in *The Listening Ear*.

Chapter 8

1. To read more on that topic see Jean Marc Eyssalet, *Dans l'Ocean des Saveurs, l'Intention du Corps – Les Cinq Chemins du Clair et de L'Obscur*, Guy Tredaniel Editeur, 1988. Unfortunately I don't know of any English translation of these admirable books. A few decades ago a group of Chinese scholars in Paris decided to retranslate the old Chinese physiology books using the original roots of these ideograms. These old texts, written with pictograms, are not conceptual but represent images of activity. They look more like poetry books.
2. The information comes from R. Hauschka in *The Nature of Substance*.
3. The Cambrian is the early earth period where some representatives of most animal phyla first appear in the fossil record. The increase of free oxygen due to plant activity must have been a major factor.
4. Steiner in 'Discussions with the Goetheanum workers', 20 Feb. 1924.

Chapter 9

1. Goethe in his *Aphorisms on Nature*, Nov. 1869.
2. A. McAllen in *The Listening Ear*.
3. Etymology of Janus in Wikipedia.
4. Steiner in *From Crystals to Crocodiles*, 13 Sept. 1922. Discussions with the workmen at the Goetheanum.
5. Steiner in his Notebooks—see Note 4 in Chapter 1.
6. Steiner in *Speech and Drama* course.
7. A. McAllen in *The Listening Ear*.
8. Kolisko in *Zoology for Everybody*, No. 8, Kolisko Archive Publication.
9. R. Hauschka in *The Nature of Substance*.

Chapter 10

1. G. J. Tortora and N. P. Anagnostakos in *Principles of Anatomy and Physiology, Centre Educatif et Culturel inc* (CEC).
2. Ibid.
3. R. Hauschka in *The Nature of Substance*.
4. A. McAllen in *The Listening Ear*.
5. A. M. McAllen in *The Listening Ear*.
6. R. Hauschka in *The Nature of Substance*.
7. Ibid.

Chapter 11

1. Steiner in *The World of the Senses and the World of the Spirit*.
2. Steiner in *Spiritual Ecology*, Dornach, 5 Jan. 1923.
3. Steiner in 'The Cycle of the Year as the Breathing Process of the Earth', lecture, April 2, 1923.
4. Wolfgang Held in *The Quality of Numbers 1 to 31*, Floris Books.
5. Ibid.
6. Wikipedia.
7. Wikipedia.
8. R. Hauschka in *The Nature of Substance*.
9. Ibid.

10. Ibid.
11. Ibid.
12. Eugen Kolisko in *Zoology for Everybody*, No. 4.
13. A. McAllen in *The Listening Ear*.
14. Ibid.
15. R. Steiner, Munich, 1908.
16. Jean-Marc Eyssalet in *Les Cinq Chemins du Clair et de l'Obscur*, Guy Tredaniel, Editeur.
17. Victor Bott, Paul Coroze and Ernst Marti treat this in depth in their book *The Forces of Life*, Centre Triades, 1981.
18. Steiner in *The Wrong and the Right Use of Esoteric Knowledge*, Lect. 3, Nov. 1917, GA 178.
19. R. Hauschka in *The Nature of Substance*.

Chapter 12

1. Steiner in *The Warmth Course*, Lecture XI, Stuttgart, 9 March, 1920.
2. Steiner in *Anthroposophy: An Introduction*, Lect. 9, Feb/March 1924.
3. Steiner in *The World of the Senses and the World of the Spirit*, 1912.
4. Wolfgang Held in *The Quality of Numbers 1 to 31*, Floris Books.
5. Ibid.
6. Walter Holtzapfel in *The Human Organs*, Lanthorn Press.
7. W. Holtzapfel in *The Human Organs*.
8. Victor Bott, Paul Coroze, Ernst Marti in *The Forces of Life*, Centre Triades. They mentioned that Steiner prefered the use of 'rhythmic unfoldment' instead of 'process'.
9. Steiner in 'Forming of Man through Cosmic Influences (Form, Life, Soul & Spirit)', Dornach, 28 Oct.–5 Nov., 1921.
10. Steiner in *Occult Physiology*.
11. Jean-Marc Eyssalet in *Shen ou L'Instant Createur* gives an overview of this important ideogram from the old Chinese medicine. *Shen* represents a power of relation, a certain way of being in the world specific to an individual.
12. James Dyson, MD in a lecture at the Economic Conference, 2016 in Folkstone, England.
13. A. McAllen in *The Listening Ear*.

14. Alice A. Bailey in *The Labours of Hercules — An Astrological Interpretation*, Lucis Press.

15. Steiner in 'Discussion with the Goetheanum's workmen', 2 Dec. 1922, from *From Comets to Cocaine...*

A note from the publisher

For more than a quarter of a century, **Temple Lodge Publishing** has made available new thought, ideas and research in the field of spiritual science.

Anthroposophy, as founded by Rudolf Steiner (1861-1925), is commonly known today through its practical applications, principally in education (Steiner-Waldorf schools) and agriculture (biodynamic food and wine). But behind this outer activity stands the core discipline of spiritual science, which continues to be developed and updated. True science can never be static and anthroposophy is living knowledge.

Our list features some of the best contemporary spiritual-scientific work available today, as well as introductory titles. So, visit us online at **www.templelodge.com** and join our emailing list for news on new titles.

If you feel like supporting our work, you can do so by buying our books or making a direct donation (we are a non-profit/charitable organisation).

office@templelodge.com

☀ TEMPLE LODGE

For the finest books of Science and Spirit